BS1415.2 .M3

THE BOOK OF JOB

The Book of Job

A Study Manual

by
ANDREW MACBEATH

BAKER BOOK HOUSE
Grand Rapids, Michigan

Library of Congress Catalog Card Number: 66-29242
Copyright, 1966, by
Baker Book House Company

ISBN: 0-8010-5900-3

First printing, December 1966
Second printing, July 1969
Third printing, March 1972
Fourth printing, July 1978

PHOTOLITHOPRINTED BY CUSHING - MALLOY, INC.
ANN ARBOR, MICHIGAN, UNITED STATES OF AMERICA
1978

To
Emmie,
Our four bairns,
and the large B. T. I. Family
scattered abroad

INTRODUCTION

A. THE READERS WHO WILL PROFIT

What a man or woman discovers in the Book of Job may prove a milestone in their life. Unique among the writings which make up the Holy Scriptures, it has an appeal so many-sided that it reaches us at all stages of our life and in whatever condition we are. Whether we are *in fellowship with God* or our soul has lost touch with Him and there is no health in us, this book will speak to our condition.

Many a converted man has fallen *out of fellowship with God.* It is the sad, familiar story—"God in the Shadows." There is perhaps an unspoken sense of grievance. The causes of the estrangement have never been honestly examined, but somehow, vaguely, the blame has been put on God.

"Oh, that I knew where I might find Him!" That cry from the tormented heart of the sufferer reaches *a heart benumbed by love of this present world,* and it causes a twinge of pain. Most of our steps forward into new faith and freedom are taken as a result of acute discomfort. And it is disturbing in the extreme if we are compelled honestly to confess that we do not want to find God —not yet! This outspoken man Job is at least determined to get through to God—am I?

The beginning of *honest thought*—how many will confess that they owe this spiritual new birth to the Book of Job!

Many people are *waiting to be in the right mood* before they begin to speak to God. What blindness of heart! Since Job's heart and his flesh cried out for the living God, he was importunate. However confused his mind was, it was *the will to be on good terms with God* that took control. He faced in the right direction and reached out toward God his groping hands.

Another large group of people begin to explore the Book of Job because *sorrow has upset them* and *life is so baffling.* Troubles never come singly, and thus many of us find ourselves waging a war on two fronts. We feel sure we are going to be overwhelmed —until we meet somebody whose plight is far worse than ours. Calamities fell thick and fast upon this old-world sufferer—so we take up the book again, and *find new courage and faith.*

Once again, *the inquiring mind of youth* is stimulated by the boldness of thought which God permits from His servant, and it is also encouraged in research, and fascinated, by the fact that when God eventually breaks through He does not come to answer questions but to ask more questions. Seeing the world in chaos because of pride and selfishness and moral cowardice and greed, eager young thinkers are in revolt against the status quo, and the adventurous Job who challenges conventional ways of thinking and is determined to find the truth becomes a hero to them. All truth must be God's truth, and Job battles on, knowing only that his goal is God. Does he sometimes seem a skeptic? That is only because, like many Christians with less skill at diagnosis, he is aware of faith in his heart but also of unbelief that lurks there (like the father in such poignant grief in Mark 9:24).

But it is not only perplexity and pain that draw us to this book. To revert to our first instances, it is *spiritual poverty*. Not backsliders alone (an alarmingly large class of Christians!) but all whose spiritual growth has been arrested require to keep company with Job. For the book is too large to have even so great a subject as suffering as its main content. It covers the entire development of our soul's life in fellowship with God. *Progress in the knowledge of God* is the grand, inclusive theme.

Whatever be the blight from which the soul has suffered during this strange, mysterious life on earth, and whatever disasters have overtaken us, the message of Job's experience is that *God is offering us better things than at our beginnings*. A well-known Scottish song gives voice to the pessimistic verdict that there can be in life "no second spring." But is it true? Job's sorrows certainly proved the seed-time out of which came golden harvests (Ps. 126:6). And such is the will of God for everyone who approaches this book with heartache. Not answers to questions (though why not that too?) but God Himself has the answer to all our deep need both in life and in death.

Not the least of the questions asked in the book takes this form: "If a man die, shall he live again?" The advances of science and the exploration of outer space are not so remote from this vital book as might be supposed. God's invitation to Job to look abroad on the vast creation (chaps. 38-41) reminds us not to be content with mere processes, but to expect a Person, God. The question of immortality arises very naturally when a man, as Job shows us, is tortured by the seeming meaninglessness of existence. But the prior question for Job was the reality of God. This he never doubted, but the contradictions and inequalities of life had driven him to the heart of the question: What sort of Being is

God? After he was confronted by God again in His unmistakable reality and grace ("God is light, and in Him is no darkness at all," 1 John 1:5), then a continuance of fellowship with Him beyond the grave is an unavoidable inference from our experience here and now.

How modern the Book is, nay, how timeless, how apt in its speech to every age and climate! How nourishing for the *saints who live under earthly tyrannies still,* and how vividly helpful to those *whose flesh is gnawed by disease* or racked with discomfort!

Best of all, the Book of Job leads by a secret stair direct to Gethsemane and Calvary. Like Jeremiah's story of loneliness on the breast of God, and like Isaiah 53, the Book of Job tells of a servant of God approved in a special degree, but because of that very approval subjected to sufferings that seem unparalleled. Therefore the whole Book is *an "unconscious prophecy" of Christ and His Cross.* Christ was par excellence, the One of whom God said, "There is none like him!" That was why God could entrust to Him the deepest, most mysterious suffering. Yet it was groping Job who uncovered the thought of incarnation and atonement, and did so just when his anguish was deepest and he cried out for a Mediator (9:32, 33).

For the Mark of Discipleship, see footnote to Chapter 19.

Well did A. B. Davidson in 1862 compare the book to "Jacob wrestling with the unknown God who finally revealed Himself and blessed him. The secrets of such a night revealed and written down compose this book of Job. And we call Job a drama because it exhibits the progress of this struggle, till its issue in the blessing. Thus it is wrong to consider the book as intended to teach any particular truth: it teaches nearly all truth. It is a life-history, a life-drama; all that is necessary for life and godliness comes to light in it."

Two things remain to be said. 1. The reader must be more than a reader: he must read *and study* the book of Job. And this will involve buying a version which shows the prose of the narrative and the poetry of the discussion as two separate things. Whereas the narrative carries the meaning on the surface, poetry tends to repeat and elaborate the thought in parallelism, and will therefore demand closer attention if the meaning is to be grasped. The English Revised Version or the American Standard Version form an essential preparation for study, and still more recent versions, too, give a better sense in Job than the Authorised Version, which is at its best in the cadences of the noblest passages but often is very obscure and disheartening elsewhere. The American Standard Version of 1901 is the one here employed and recommended. The writer counts it quite the best for Bible Translators.

2. It is fatal in the discussions of Job and his friends to read just a chapter at a time. The book is a unity and deserves concentrated attention and re-reading over quite a few chapters in sequence. We need to ask ourselves questions about each speaker's contribution, and how far it advances or beclouds the matter at issue. To the speeches of God and of Job more special attention should be given, as a master-interpreter shows:

"Incomparably the grandest and most fascinating in their simplicity and exquisite imagery are the speeches of Jehovah; for the author knew the great law, that simplicity is necessarily also sublimity. Each of Job's friends has a diction and style to some extent peculiar to himself; the greatest mastery over the language, and the greatest riches of thought, being exhibited in Job's speeches, not far behind whom in both is Eliphaz, whose first discourse is a masterpiece of argumentation on the relations of man and God, as Job's last is a masterpiece of delineation of the extent of human ignorance here and human woe" (A . B. Davidson, *A Commentary on Job* Vol. I, 1862).

B. THE BOOK AND ITS SPECIAL FEATURES

ITS AGE AND BACKGROUND. The scene depicted inside the book is patriarchal. Wealth is estimated by cattle; the head of the family acts as priest. The names used of God are El, Eloah and Shaddai, in that order of frequency (total occurrences 127). The covenant name Jehovah is restricted in use to the Prologue, God's speeches and the Epilogue, except for 12:9 and 28:28 (30 times in all). It seems that Job is chosen as representative man, to show the message of the book as universal. There is no reference to Israel's privileges, to Mosaic Law or priesthood, special sacrifice or Temple, and no awareness of Israel's deeply significant history.

The life story of Job is ancient and widely known (Ezek. 14:14; James 5:11). In Matthew 24:28 our Lord shows knowledge of Job 39:30. When it was that this grand story was so magnificently treated and made available for God's people, we do not know. In its own way the book is a kind of Melchizedec (a man outside of Israel, a pattern of godliness is its hero) for it appears without ancestors and has no descendants. What a gap there would be in the Canon if it were not there! How remarkable the fact that it was ever included there, associated as it was with Esau's descendants, the people who earned such bitter dislike from the Jews when Jerusalem fell at the hands of the Chaldeans!

JOB IS A WISDOM BOOK, BUT ITS THEME IS THEOLOGICAL.

Edom became renowned for its wisdom and wise men. In Solomon's time there arose groups of men who developed separately from the prophets who were Israel's distinctive glory as messengers of God. The prophets interpreted on the scale of the nation as a whole the dealings of God in reward and punishment. National greatness or the nation's decline and fall were interpreted, and rightly so, on the narrow alternatives of fidelity to their God or apostasy from His covenant grace. Jeremiah and Ezekiel had the task of applying to individual cases the rulings of God about corporate retribution, or solidarity in sin, which showed children as paying the penalty for sins of their fathers (Ezek. 18). This attempt of the prophets to penetrate the mysteries of suffering as it bears on the godly is very striking. (cp. Jer. 12:1; Hab. 1:13). Says Strahan of the prophets, "Their doubt was faith perplexed, faith tried, faith bewildered, faith tortured." How remarkable that from a different camp altogether, that of Wisdom, issues a book which unites with Jeremiah and the Servant passages in Isaiah 42-53 to give flesh and blood to the portrait of a Sufferer beyond all others who must also wait before He can see of the travail of His soul!

Davidson in 1862 wrote, "Job, out of his religious entanglement, proclaimed the necessity of a mediator to humanize God. What man needs is God to take man's part against God. Thus, like fountains in the desert, bubble forth, all over this dreary pilgrimage of Job, those clear springs of christology." Adds Terrien, "For a Semite, a prince of monotheism, this is a stupendous thought."

When the book of Job was written, we cannot tell, nor who was the author. What matters is the revelation and the reticence, the solace after the struggle, and the mysterious sustaining of the soul even when the soul feels its burden of loneliness and restlessness to be intolerable. (Ps. 63:8).

After we have heard outspoken Job lashing out against an

Adversary, a dark, arbitrary, heavenly Antagonist, we are the more impressed when the Son of His love makes this the first petition in the prayer given to His disciples: "Our Father, which art in heaven, *hallowed be Thy name*." It was for the hallowing of that Name, as P. T. Forsyth often showed, that Christ trod the way of the cross. It was because Jesus knew the sovereignty of God to be "absolute sovereignty, with the right to make demand on man and no reason given, and no light shown on the spot" that He exclaimed in an hour of set-back, "Even so, Father, so it hath seemed good in Thy sight" (Matt. 11:26).

What Job craved for, a sovereignty that was not merely of wisdom and of power, but of righteousness with peace and joy as its attendants, was what the Son of God brought to light (Rom. 14:17). So great, so central was the issue on which Job's troubled mind was impaled—the character of God. That such an awakened, sternly demanding soul as Job's was *satisfied*— that is the measure of the encounter with God at the end as carrying everything that Job cried out for, and much more.

Other important features of the Book's message will be shown within the commentary, at the Book's turning-points.

BIBLIOGRAPHY

Holy Bible: American Standard Version 1901
    A Modern Translation
Davidson, A. B., *Commentary grammatical and exegetical on the Book of Job*. Vol. I (chaps. 1-14). Williams and Norgate, London, 1862.
―――――, Job in *The Cambridge Bible*. 1884 and later editions.
Dhorme, *Le Livre de Job*. Deuxieme Edition. Librairie Victor Lecoffre, 1926.
Driver, S. R., & George Buchanan Gray, *A Critical and Exegetical Commentary on The Book of Job*. (I.C.C.). T. & T. Clark, Edinburgh, 1921.
Green, William Henry, *The Argument of the Book of Job Unfolded*. Robert Carter & Bros. New York, 1881.
Heavenor, E. S. P., *The Book of Job*, "The New Bible Commentary." Inter-Varsity Fellowship, London.
Irwin, W. J., *The Book of Job*, "Peake's Commentary on the Bible." (Revised and reset). Thomas Nelson Company, Ltd., London & Edinburgh, 1962.
Kelly, B. H., *Ezra to Job*, "The Layman's Bible Commentaries." S.C.M. Press Ltd., London.
McFadyen, *The Problem of Pain*, James Clark & Co., London, nd.

Peake, A. S., *The Book of Job,* Century Bible. T. C. & E. C. Jack, Edinburgh, 1904.

Robinson, H. Wheeler, *The Cross of Job.* S.C.M. Press Ltd., London, 1916.

Strahan, James, *The Book of Job Interpreted.* T. & T. Clark, Edinburgh, 1914.

Terrien, Samuel, *Interpreter's Bible,* Vol. 3, 1954.

—————, *Job: Commentaire de l'A.T.*, Delachaux & Niestle, Neuchatel, 1963.

THE STRUCTURE OF THE BOOK OF JOB

I. PROLOGUE: The Basic Story with Scenes in Heaven and on Earth, Chapters 1, 2

II. JOB'S COMPLAINT, Chapter 3

III. THE DISCUSSION, Chapters 4-27
    A. First Cycle of Discussion, Chapters 4-14
        1. Eliphaz, Chapters 4, 5
        2. Job, Chapters 6, 7
        3. Bildad, Chapter 8
        4. Job, Chapters 9, 10
        5. Zophar, Chapter 11
        6. Job Replies, Chapters 12-14
    B. Second Cycle of Discussion, Chapters 15-21
        1. Eliphaz, Chapter 15
        2. Job, Chapters 16, 17
        3. Bildad, Chapter 18
        4. Job, Chapter 19
        5. Zophar, Chapter 20
        6. Job Replies, Chapter 21
    C. Third Cycle of Discussion, Chapters 22-27
        1. Eliphaz, Chapter 22
        2. Job, Chapters 23, 24
        3. Bildad, Chapter 25
        4. Job Replies, Chapters 26, 27

IV. INTERLUDE: IN PRAISE OF WISDOM, Chapter 28

V. JOB'S FINAL SPEECH, Chapters 29-31
        1. The Past Recalled, Chapter 29
        2. The Present Surveyed, Chapter 30
        3. The Oath and Summing Up, Chapter 31

VI. THE INTERVENTION OF ELIHU, Chapters 32-37

VII. GOD SPEAKS OUT OF THE WHIRLWIND, Chapters 38-42:6

VIII. EPILOGUE ON EARTH, Chapter 42:7-17

COMMENTARY ON THE BOOK OF JOB

A DRAMATIC STORY OF UPHEAVAL, Chapter 1

This story begins where other stories of the great narrative tradition used to end. A bright boy, his early struggle and hardships, the courage he showed and how he won through to sure success and family joys—such has always been the pattern of popular stories. In the course of these biographies or romances we were made spectators of an unfolding drama. We were watching first the formation of character until with the passing years there came honor, substance, and public esteem.

At once we become aware that the Book of Job is different. From the very first verse we are confronted by a man whose character is already mature. So rounded off, so marked by integrity is this man that the opening description of him is twice confirmed from the lips of God Himself, at 1:8 and 2:3. No man in the Old Testament is portrayed as sinless or faultless, but thrice over Job is declared to be blameless and upright. So unusual is this situation that we begin to realise that this is precisely the setting of the big problem.

This overture (as musicians would call it) in the first five verses, is an ideal scene of earthly peace and happiness. Yet it is no dreamland story, for two striking down-to-earth features of the hero are described. The first was reverent, worshipping awareness of God—he *feared God*—and besides he was constantly alert and watchful to give sin a wide berth: he *turned away from evil*.

Character—that is the word that springs to our mind as we observe the build-up of the story in its first sentence. Job was a man of unusual character. This is more impressive when we note the locality from which he comes. Hebrew scholars will notice this in the first two words, in an order different from the one that is usual when linking up an Israelite with the traditions and institutions of his race. Job, you see, is unconnected with the chosen people. He is selected from without the history of God's dealings with Israel. He comes from *the land of Uz,* and we know this area was on the border of the Edomites, and the Edomites had a reputation for wisdom. This is worth remembering when we come to listen to the speeches of Job's three friends:

they represent the best "wisdom" of their time, yet there is no racial or religious prejudice. The book speaks a universal language.

After a description of the character of Job we are next informed about his prosperity and then about his piety.

Job's possessions are what would nowadays be described as fabulous. What a ranch! What trading caravans of laden camels going like Marco Polo to exotic Oriental courts and markets! What cultivation of prairies to meet the human pressures and to feed the hungry! We are not surprised to learn that this man who was so good was also great. He was the greatest or richest of all the people of the east (v. 3).

Yet the crowning quality about Job was shown in what he was at home. He was pre-eminent for his piety. Not so many men who have made a success as merchants, farmers, or stock-raisers have been a success with their own children. But Job was. What made Job rise early was not market prices nor stocks, but the true welfare of his large and very happy family. A man "watchful unto prayer"—that was Job. His concern was not merely to enforce a certain code of morals upon the young. He was eager to secure a healthy attitude of soul *toward God*. Individual shepherding of his own children seems to be the meaning of verse 5, which says that *he would send* (for them) *and sanctify them*. He engaged with them in some act of confession, cleansing, and prayer. Job took a serious view of sin: he acted as the family's priest, and offered an atoning sacrifice for sin (which is named as the whole burnt offering).

Such was the setting of this good man's life, described in what may be called the Overture. So far, peace reigns.

From a peaceful scene on earth we are transported at verse 6 to the heavenly court. God is hearing reports from His angels. Among them duly appears "the Satan" (as yet this is a title, not a proper name). He is not yet described as the ruler of a rival empire, nor conceived as having withdrawn from the service of God. Whatever further light the Scriptures will in future cast upon him, especially in his conflict with God's Anointed One, it is comforting to be reminded meantime that Satan has his limitations, always.

The function of the angels seems to be that of assessors or examiners. Quite rightly it is expected that only those on earth who have clean hands and a pure heart should find access to God's holy hill. The angels and the Satan are not to treat lightly the true qualifications needed for drawing near to the Holy

One. While the angels pass in review what they have observed on earth, God singles out Job as a man unique. There is "none like him." We must notice at this point what might pass us by if we brought a full-grown doctrine of Satan to this passage. The striking thing is that Satan objects to the approval God bestows on Job and objects on the plea that Job at heart may be nothing but a worshipper of Mammon. "Doth Job fear God for nought?" (v. 9). The answer to this question is the Book's theme. Satan suggests that "his house and *all that he has*" are the dominating interest in Job's life (v. 11). Meanwhile God has permitted Satan to deal as he pleases with "all that Job has," and Satan seems confident about success. So Satan went forth from the presence of the LORD (v. 12). Note the name, the Lord, Jehovah: Israel's covenant name for God is used in the Prologue, those first two chapters which supply the author's own explanation of that mystery which throughout the rest of the book will be so baffling to Job himself—so baffling as to involve torment of soul.

At verse 13 our viewing is switched back from heaven to earth. Never was such a swift succession of catastrophes recorded in such brief and vivid words. We pause and say to ourselves: All that is now happening is within the permissive will of God. It is breathtaking. To anyone but a man of faith it would be overwhelming. Stroke upon stroke of calamity comes: twice by the violence of men, and twice by what lawyers call an "act of God." Palpitatingly the messengers tell each their woeful tale. The repetition of the news by "formula" imparts an element of naked horror to the story, and each time the verdict, apart from one sole messenger, is "total loss."

Swift incursions of wild men from the desert and of Chaldeans in more strictly military formations, and lightning that burned up sheep and servants together indiscriminatingly (cp. Luke 13: 1), and last of all a pitiless hurricane which laid all his ten children dead—this is the astonishing recitative.

And then come the majestic words that describe how Job "took it," and later what he said. No wonder his words have found their way into the Anglican Book of Common Prayer, and are repeated at every Christian burial service! "Then Job arose, and rent his robe, and shaved his head [all artificial additions of clothing and even hair were removed as possible sources of pride], and he fell on the ground and worshipped; and he said, Naked came I out of my mother's womb, and naked shall I return thither: the LORD gave, and the LORD hath taken away; blessed be the name of the LORD."

Job was like Abraham ascending Mt. Moriah and reckoning that God had a perfect right to recall the miracle son Isaac whom He had given. Job recognised God's ownership of the children and of all the other possessions of Job. He did not ascribe to God any action unworthy of Himself—he "thought magnificently of God," was truly adoring and worshipful. What a summit of faith and reverence!

THE SECOND COURT SCENE IN HEAVEN, 2:1-6

"Unabashed," as Strahan puts it, Satan appears a second time when God's examiners of men are giving their reports. Once again Satan only possesses the right to say or suggest anything when he is directly interrogated by his King. To the general and then a particular inquiry about his doings, Satan is given leave to speak, but first God seeks to lead Satan to right thinking by showing the splendid quality of Job's faith when adversity had stripped him bare. God had been vindicated. But Satan (this one who pretends so assiduously to be our friend!) again has doubts about the best of men. God had been vindicated, although this Holy One, in the manner of Scripture familiar to its greatest lovers, is almost depicted in naive human fashion as coming near regretting the action He took ("Thou movedst me against him," v. 3). Job, says God, "still holds fast his integrity" (v. 3).

God sees Job as a man who is all of a piece, crystal clear, a man who is going in one direction with all his might. Integrity is this wholeness, this singleness and not doubleness of aim, which God counts fundamental! But once again Satan disagrees. At heart Job is a pitiless egotist, says Satan. The skin of his ten children matters little so long as his own skin is intact. But let his bones be racked and his flesh quiver with pain, and then see how he reacts!

The wise writer of this holy Book unashamedly puts down the statement that God said to Satan, "Behold, he is in your power; only spare his life" (v. 6). Everything is traced back to the action and permission of God. Job believes that, and we shall see how it torments him. But a true faith is often purified in the furnace of affliction. A faith worth having is only made victorious and serene when a man or woman has been "emptied from vessel to vessel" (Jer. 48:11). We shall believe this more fully after studying this book, and our conviction of God's sovereign control will bring deeper peace. Peace, even when we cannot explain. We must remember that the explanation here made known to us is hidden from Job. The genuineness of his faith is being tested. Note in passing that explanations are not given in our Bible to satisfy mere curiosity, or to encourage men's speculations about God's ways (Deut. 29:29).

We need to remind ourselves that the scenes in Heaven are given a parabolic cast, or dramatically conceived, as in Micaiah's parable to King Ahab in 1 Kings 22. The point is that these scenes in heaven are not to be scrutinised or interpreted with relentless logic. For all who have eyes to see, the writer of Job is a perfect seer. His message is like the light from an unflickering lamp: here it is: What He permits to happen to Job, God will "stand for." The Bible says that God does not willingly afflict or grieve the children of men (Lam. 3:33). God's wisdom and love can be trusted. In a world where cancer and other painful scourges are familiar facts, dedicated research workers ceaselessly strive to dispel their power. This form of co-operation from man's side is part of God's intention. Meantime we only know part of the reason why God permits suffering. One day we shall clearly see. God will be vindicated. By its reticence in explaining things, yet by its suggestions of a true repose which even now true faith possesses, this Book of Job is pure gold. By insights such as this chapter gives, a novice in faith can become a mature believer, and the genuine man of faith will glorify God increasingly through testing, as he comes to know God better and learns more from life. His best tribute of praise is given when he stands up to distress and anguish in the way God's beloved Son endured the Cross, despising shame. Yes, Job was allowed to suffer in his bones and in his flesh. Was Satan a materialist here? It will later become plain that an unconquerable certainty about God is able to lift a man or woman clear above the sharpest agony of bodily pain. Not pain in bone or flesh could break Job. His need was for faith to be nurtured and made triumphant.

LOATHSOME SORES, BUT A MORE ACUTE PAIN THAN THESE, 2:7-9

There are no half-measures, so the Bible states very plainly. The second hurricane of calamity now swept over Job. "From the sole of his foot to the crown of his head," Job has loathsome sores. Outside the village, on the heap where garbage is cast, Job sits where he is recognised as being in quarantine. What mental suffering this involved we shall see in the Dialogue and later in Chapter 30. "Among the ashes"—what a location for this once king of men!

But what cut him to the heart was that his wife in her sheer loyalty and affection for him suffered a terrible landslide in faith (v. 9). She "went with the multitude." The thoughts of God that she admitted to her mind were cheap and mean. "Renounce God" and get the story finished finally in your death (v. 9)! This is the egocentric view. She was the last one left to her husband! Almost the final string on hope's lyre was gone! But with the dignity and authority of the best husband the Bible has depicted Job replies: "Shall we receive good at the hand of God, and shall we not receive evil?" Here indeed was a man who did not sin against God with his lips nor in his secret heart. Not self but God is at the center.

AN APPOINTMENT TO VISIT JOB BY THREE FRIENDS, 2:11-13

After this deeply impressive account of Job's unshaken trust in God through two successive hurricanes of trouble, a transition is made at 2:11. From the hero's lonely battleground where he stood indomitable to the last, we come to the company of sympathising friends. Strange to relate, Job is now "in the arena"— an arena where he writhes in anguish as though a wild bull was twisting its horns in his very bowels. Dignified, sympathetic, silently seated near him through seven days, these men were appalled at the change in his situation and in his appearance. "They raised their voices and wept," as Orientals are more prone to do than the Anglo-Saxon race. Speech would have seemed an impertinence, for "they saw that his suffering was very great." Their grief was genuine. They came to express their grief and to comfort their friend.

FORECAST OF THE DEBATE

Here ends the short, vivid old-world story of the "patience" of Job. With Chapter 3 we enter upon that debate with his friends in which a main feature will be his passionate impatience with their theories and pleas and arguments. Despite their long and reverential silence through seven days and the courteous opening words of Eliphaz, there seemed to be after Job's wild outburst something stony in their attitude which repelled, discouraged and exasperated him. The unfolding is of intense, if painful, interest.

Besides this, Job is also shown as a wrestler in the strangle-hold of a baffling mystery. For the moment may we call it the mystery of knowing God and yet not knowing Him, of loving yet not loving Him? Nowhere is uncertainty so tormenting and intolerable as uncertainty about God. Yet grief takes toll. Was nervous exhaustion one big factor in his reaction?

We are to make it our business to study Job's deep unrest of spirit and also the methods of his friends in their attempt to help and heal. Why did they fail?

For the student eager to derive most profit from this deep and enthralling book, two suggestions may be made.

1. We must note how central God is in all Job's distress. He has been the supreme reality in all Job's life, but suddenly His ways have become a mystery. We shall observe closely all that Job says, for how can a man stand up to life unless he has got through to God and knows Him well?

Here a Christian reader must beware of reading into Job's mind the full acquaintance with God that has come to us in Christ. The true light is now shining for us, writes the Apostle John. The full revelation of the Father had to wait for the coming of God's Son (Heb. 1:1, 2). We ought therefore patiently to listen and consider, also taking if we can the attitude of a physician who is longing to lead the sufferer back to vigorous health of soul. Instead of being alarmed or censorious at the too free utterance of doubts, we need to watch the writhings of a soul in order to be skilful when we apply faith's remedy to others.

2. In studying the speeches of the friends, it is fascinating to do this in two ways. First, we should compare speaker with speaker, character with character. Eliphaz, Bildad, and Zophar each has marked individuality of manner and approach—and later Elihu has a character of his own. Second, we should watch the progress or development of any one speaker as the debate advances. For instance Eliphaz should be closely observed in his speeches, the first in Chapters 4 and 5, the second in Chapter 15, and the third in Chapter 22. Dignified and courteous as Eliphaz was in his opening speech, making his charges vaguely and indirectly, he departs from mere generalities in his third speech. He becomes fiercely specific there. It is of interest also to note how all three take pains to describe the miseries that befall the wicked man, hoping they may compel Job to discern his own portrait in the description, or at least take warning and turn back penitently to God. Especially in the second cycle of speeches, from 15:20, 18:5 and 20:4 onwards, note this theme.

At times, however, each one is pointedly personal, for with every speech that Job makes their alienation from him grows, and their distrust of him. Finally they "believe him to have been secretly guilty of the most atrocious and outrageous crimes" (W. H. Green).

Eventually these two lines of study must be brought together. A careful progressive study of Job's anguish of mind must be interwoven with the provocation he receives from the unfeeling, perverse and pitiless theorizings of his friends. Is it not their unfairness in pleading the cause of God which distorts the image of the character of God for Job? Granted that sinfulness is common to all men, have they shown the reason "why one man is singled out rather than another and made to endure extraordinary sorrows?" The God whom Job has known in the past, and whom in the future he will know again, is really God, but that God with whom the friends torment him in the present seems, as Peake says, "a spectre of his morbid imagination." From deep places of despair, Job is sometimes lifted to a momentary glimpse of God as his Vindicator. Like many another he is saved by hope, as though God bears him aloft on eagles' wings (cp. Exod. 19:4).

After Job's final speeches in Chapters 29-31, a young man intervenes, Elihu by name. At the right place we shall examine Chapters 33-37 and see how far he makes good the inadequate instruction given by the older men. There all debate ends.

Then it was that the Lord answered Job out of the whirlwind. From Chapters 38-41 comes God's surprising answer. Last of all, we read Job's words of surrender and adoration, and the epilogue is a story of new beginnings which make a perfect ending.

JOB'S STRANGE OUTBURST OF COMPLAINT, Chapter 3

After the prose narrative of the Prologue in Chapters 1 and 2, the "Debate" proceeds in Hebrew poetry whose chief feature is that each statement is repeated or elaborated a second time. The thoughts expressed are also given a variety of dress or imagery, just as musicians repeat phrases and themes but interweave and diversify them. Job's complaint about life as travail (v. 10), and "raging" like a furious sea in verse 17 (cp. Isa. 57:20), or torment and unremitting agony in verse 26, is conveyed in the language of emotion rather than of reason, that is, in poetry. We are meant to *feel* with the speaker. As Job will later protest at 6:3, his words have been rash and quite inadequate (so the failure of his friends to take soundings in his grief would indicate), and his friends might have been expected to make allowances for the overflow of sorrow from his surcharged heart. In his mind the contrast between his own anguished unrest and the seeming quietness of the grave stands out as intolerable. He invests the realm of those asleep with every grace, using no less than four verbs in verse 13, and coming back upon the attractions of quietness in verse 17, only to conclude at verse 26 with his own agitated condition—"I am not at ease, neither am I quiet, neither have I rest."

The three main things Job seems to say are that his birth was a disaster (1-10); only death is desirable (11-19); why then is light given to him, when it only intensifies the contradiction of his lost, benighted condition (20-26)? The three parts of his speech also include 1-10, Job's Curse; 11-19, His Questions; 20-26, His Complaint.

In section (1) from verses 1-10 the reader moving from the majestic Chapter 2 is ill-prepared for this outburst from Job's lips. Almost we can excuse the three friends for starting off on the wrong foot. Yet Job's nervous exhaustion plus something in their demeanor must be the explanation for his despair.

Of course, we are compelled to ask, What pastor takes so seriously the first rush of grief from a mourner? Does any man of tender heart argue phrase by phrase with what a widow says in the paroxysms of early bereavement? (Paroxysm, remember, is the thought behind the word for "trouble" in vv. 10, 17, 26.) Job is losing taste for life.

Strange! A godly man finds fault with God, and wishes that his birthday might be mentioned not with congratulations but with a curse! We know that Jeremiah was driven to the same extremity of despondency (Jer. 20:14-18). The very thought of light arising and the dawn breaking on that day when he was born is offensive to the distracted man, for that day was the beginning of sorrows (vv. 5-9). The long happy years are meantime forgotten, for pessimism once it finds expression knows no measure. Job's fancy dwells for a moment on the thought that sorcerers, or some primeval dragon, or Leviathan, might have the power to cause an eclipse and get that day blotted out from the calendar (v. 8).

"If only I might never have been!" This thought is given great solemnity by our Saviour when He speaks about such a man as Judas Iscariot. Matthew Henry therefore is right in suggesting that Job's language is only appropriate to the remorse of a man in hell. Compared with unavailing remorse, a sorrow such as Job expresses is sharp and keen because it is too self-conscious, or one might say because it is entirely *self*-conscious. That, as we see later, was precisely to what his friends drove him. What Augustine referred to as our human failing beyond all others, the lust for self-vindication, is the place at which Job like all of us is so vulnerable. The standing we have in God's sight is not enough for us: we want to stand well before our neighbors and before the saints! Many of us with far less of catastrophe than Job had to cope with are all too prone to give ourselves an overdose of misery when what is at stake is not the honor of God, and not our own integrity, but just our fancied prestige. What a mercy it is for us of the Christian era that we can go to dark Gethsemane and there forget our sorrow and our fancied pain!

Job was completely shut in with the present and the past. He sees no future. In section (2), from verses 11-19, he dreams of a realm of quiet rest, of lying down and sleeping in entire unconsciousness.

Meanwhile for Job consciousness is only consciousness of pain. Absorbed with that, he asks why consciousness should ever have had a beginning. "Why did I not die at birth?" (v. 11). Then he recalls a custom: when a child was born, it was deposited upon the knees of its father. Later the child was brought close to the breasts of its mother. Why was that quivering little thing received with joy, only to be later made susceptible to sorrow? Then Job's mind thinks of the inequalities of life, and he sees pass in procession the kings and the counsellors, the rich and the poor, the prisoner and his warder, the small and the great, the slave and his master. Where, he asks, does all this up and down, this high and low, end? Of course, it ends in the grave. Death is the great leveller. With this thought he seems to think the attraction of Sheol is enhanced—Sheol, the dim underworld where the wicked cease from troubling, and all are on a level. Keats too, knowing that disease was bringing on a premature death, was moved by a nightingale's song to dream that he might "cease upon the midnight, with no pain." But Keats did not shut half of the truth from himself as Job here does: all the later poet could say was "I am half in love with easeful death!" Says Job, "There the weary are at rest." (v. 17).

"Things present" were allowed to obscure Job's view. Supersensitive in his despondency, he concluded that he had no future. Yet it was through another man who suffered just like Job, innocently, a man, too, who just like Job wished that he had never been born, namely Jeremiah, that God declared His innermost heart in very precious words: "For I know the thoughts that I think toward you, saith the LORD, thoughts of peace and not of evil, to give you a future and a hope" (Jer. 29:11. The last phrase is from the R.S.V.).

Here lies the source of Job's temporary malady. No man can really live unless he sees himself as having a future. A man like Paul had trouble in plenty, yet hope never failed him. Paul never knew Job's bitterness. Even this Book of Job stands within the inspired volume so that we who read may profit, and our profit lies in hopefulness (see Rom. 15:4, 13). Things present cannot separate us from the love of God. After the Resurrection of Christ despondency like that of Job must be for ever ruled out (Rom. 8:35-39). Job, without knowing it, did have a future and a hope.

Chapter 3 is full of Job's Why? and Wherefore? Section (3) begins with the word again at verse 20, and gives the key question of the chapter: Why is light given when it only accentuates a sufferer's misery? In Job's thinking, light appears to be equivalent to life or sensitivity, the capacity for feeling pain and frustration. Job longs for death, and says that those with bitterness in their soul would dig for death as eagerly as miners dig for gold (v. 21). Yet we are struck by the fact that devout souls can never in the Bible contemplate ending life by their own act. What Job says in verse 22 is an excess of pessimism, however. Few would welcome death even in dire straits. Job has forgotten in his all too realistic fears (v. 25), that there is another fear, a shapeless fear, which haunts the minds of men: the fear of what comes after death—the Judgment.

Is it a permissible thought that Job perhaps had so lived all his life long in alert awareness of the judgment of God that for the moment, in his emergency, he was not a safe guide for others? Be that as it may, Job's last sentence is full of the unrest that we find in Romans 7. Verse 26 is an unquiet verse just because it is echoing with "I," "I," "I."

And it is at this point that Eliphaz begins what will prove a long, and for Job, an increasingly distressful debate. Strictly speaking the word "debate" is misleading. In a modern debate the participants give close attention to what their opponents have said and seek to answer or refute it point by point. If we analyse carefully the discussion between Job and those who one by one come forward to answer him, we shall find no such keen argumentation. Their failure here increases the attraction of the skilful delineation of the character of each. It also brings out Job's impatience with them, sometimes his almost contemptuous disregard for what they are saying. "Wrong prescription, wrong patient!" is what a modern Job would mutter under his breath. Also the intervention of young and bustling Elihu at a later stage becomes more spicy because of these shortcomings in those alleged to be "wise."

VENERABLE ELIPHAZ ELOQUENTLY SPEAKS, Chapter 4

4:1-6. You have been so helpful to others in distress: dare I attempt to recall you to your former attitude?
7-11. Your outcry is impenitent. No innocent man succumbs to trouble. Trouble discloses who really are wicked, and God swiftly dispatches them.
12-21. So majestic and pure is God (this I once learned in a breath-taking vision) that no man, not even an angel, could have any standing before him as just or clean.

Compelled by the surprise of finding Job breaking down at the onset of trouble (the dimensions of it none of the friends has taken in, except to draw the wrong conclusions), Eliphaz speaks. Gracious reference is made to the ministry Job had himself exercised in comforting many (vv. 3, 4). But at once sharp correction is offered for his loss of nerve (v. 5). It has been well said, "One would really suppose Job to have broken down at the first taste of trouble!"

Eliphaz has begun kindly, but a rebuke is mingled with the courtesy. This loss of nerve shown when Job broke out into speech, not naming God but speaking so impatiently about God's ways with him, makes the noble friend fear the worst. Therefore dignified Eliphaz probes the conscience of his friend. A God-fearing life gives hope of a happy issue from trouble—surely this is the comfort that Job has offered to other sufferers (this will be brought home at v. 7). This loss of nerve therefore seems inconceivable if a man's "fear of God" and his "integrity" are genuine (vv. 5, 6).

Inspired by considerate friendliness, Eliphaz has spoken words in which there lurks a hidden insult, as Job sees it. The venom is more biting from verse 7 onward. Suppose that Job truly is innocent: then it is impossible that he should ever perish ("perish" is the key word), for that is the sure destiny which God marks out for workers of iniquity, lions though they be in strength and pride, (vv. 8-11). Indirectly and by insinuation it has been conveyed to the sufferer that from the ruin of his fortunes his friend surmises the cause to be a secret moral collapse. Something has been committed which claimed nothing less than the blast of God's anger (v. 9).

Like an elder investigating a case of church discipline and not expecting to be told the truth, Eliphaz plunges on, yet mingles delicacy with his bludgeoning. The bludgeoning comes in the too startling and tactless picture of verse 11: "The old lion perisheth for lack of prey, and the whelps of the lioness (Job's children, this appears to mean!) are scattered abroad." That this is the stern moralist's meaning seems reinforced by what he will say at 5:4.

Was a sign of sharp dismay evident on Job's face at this? Like a man who has got rid of the cutting sentence he has long meditated, Eliphaz now turns to more objective exhortation (vv. 12-21). Like a musician who has been playing from the wrong score altogether, he notes that his audience is restive, so he introduces his favorite piece. In a delicate strain he will no longer describe Job as a monster of hypocrisy found out, but will describe a midnight revelation, an experience of deep solemnity granted to him. Impressively he describes the occasion (vv. 12-16). In the stillness of night, "when deep sleep falleth on men, fear came upon me and trembling which made all my bones to shake" (vv. 13, 14). In this uncanny time, stirred to panic, there passed before his face—what exactly was it? *"It stood still"*—there is suspense, and also mystery. The "it," says Peake, "creates a far more powerful impression than if Eliphaz had named it. It is unnamed because it is unknown, and thus the vagueness, which characterises the description, here also heightens the terror." The hair of his flesh stood up. All this had happened "secretly," in a whisper (v. 13), and a form was before his eyes (v. 16).

What then was the revelation from the unseen world? It is a condemnation of mortal man, and of the angels too, as being impure before man's Maker. The transcendent, holy God charges with folly the very angels. Why then should a man, framed like brittle, impermanent clay, fashioned out of dust, have any pretensions? Is he not as ephemeral as the moth (vv. 18-20), or a nomad's tent?

Softening the blow directed at Job's conscience in verses 7-11, Eliphaz treats mankind in general as incapable of self-defense, unworthy almost of consideration (but he will rectify this in chap. 5). The gap Eliphaz opens and widens, however, is a gap which God has shown Himself eager to close. All the stage-effects and dramatic power of Eliphaz, with his high principles and good intentions, are very unlike a prophet's true work after a desolation has been wrought. Like many an eloquent preacher, Eliphaz hitherto has been a failure. Yet God marked a certain nobility of mind in him and at the close took pains that Eliphaz should not himself meet the fate he described in 4:21 and "die without wisdom."

Meantime he has something further both stern and gracious, both menacing and alluring, to say in Chapter 5.

ELIPHAZ: MAGNIFICENT BUT MISDIRECTED, Chapter 5

5:1-7. How foolish a man is who thinks to withstand God; man, impure, born into trouble! Sons and all perish through a fool's folly.

8-16. This majestic God who overturns the crafty is yet kind to the penitent. I commend to you a penitent approach to God.

17-27. What a blissful prospect opens before a penitent and teachable man, with God's chastening yielding fullest peace and a large posterity!

After the claim to awe-inspiring authority from direct revelation, Eliphaz turns from the perfections of the Divine nature to frail man and the folly which makes the common human lot one of affliction and distress. This is all the direct and inevitable consequence of sinfulness. Sin and sorrow are like cause and effect. Pursuing the thought in 4:18 that even the heavenly ones, the angels, are tainted, he asks how any of them could be expected to sponsor Job if he planned to make an appeal against God. They would not intervene, knowing the gulf that separates them and Job from deity's unapproachable purity.

Clearing the ground, however, before he goes on to rhapsodise about God and his Godlikeness, Eliphaz rebukes the "vexation" or passionate heat with which Job has reacted against God's dealings with him (v. 2). The two main characteristics of the fool have been exhibited in his demeanor, the way he rejects correction and instruction, and the angry impatience he so openly expresses.

At this point (vv. 3-5), Eliphaz gives the reins to his imagination and in depicting the fool's sudden reversal of fortune comes perilously near describing Job's own domestic tragedy in terms of indelicate vividness (v. 4). The "fool" is so offensive to the soul of Eliphaz that he goes on to describe the stealing of his harvest by the hungry poor, despite the fence or covering of thorns in which he trusts (v. 5). Thus upheaval and loss are the sure plight of men, the working out of their destiny. It is something they draw upon themselves by their inherent wrongness. Indeed it is their birthright. This, and not the pathos of it, is the meaning of the words, "Man is born unto trouble as the sparks fly upward." It is the mounting flame which carries the sparks. Likewise it is man's evil nature that brings affliction. Trouble is not fortuitous nor self-generated (v. 6).

At the close of the debate, when God intervenes He will rebuke the friends for the one-sidedness and faultiness of their teaching, and commentators have indicated the source of their failure as being "a defective character rather than an erroneous theory." This is specially remarkable in the first speaker, for he kindles and glows whenever God is his theme (see especially 4:17; 5:8 and 5:18 with their following verses). "But as for me, I would seek unto God, and unto God would I commit my cause" (v. 8). The lofty attributes of God are dwelt on, yet His transcendence never involves aloofness, for He is shown in action, doing great things and unsearchable, marvellous things without number. He keeps the earth green and fruitful with rain and shows special care for those who are lowly and those who mourn—the kind of people whom our Lord will describe in the Beatitudes. The other aspect of this active God is His concern to deliver the meek from the guile and oppression of crafty exploiters. The fatherless and the poor are preserved by Him from injustice (vv. 12-16).

"Behold, happy is the man whom God correcteth." From verse 17 to the end of his speech Eliphaz aims to come close to Job's plight. His plea has always been that Job should confess his guilt, and let God heal the wounds He has inflicted, and thereafter lead the penitent into a blessed security—a security of such quality that Eliphaz needs a crescendo of poetic beauty to describe it. Immune from famine, war, and wild beasts, Job would be in tune with Nature, have many children and die in ripe old age. At peace with God, Job would be at peace with animate and inanimate nature. The one aspect of safety and peace not yet mentioned is "the scourge of the tongue" at verse 21. Commentators seem to steer past this, and some emend the Hebrew text in favor of "pestilence," having in mind the fourth of Ezekiel's "sore judgments" (Ezek. 14:21). The Dominican scholar Dhorme is surely right in discerning the appropriateness of associating "the power of the sword" and "the scourge of the tongue," for the tongue can inflict as deadly a wound as any sword. Besides, there is assonance in the Hebrew words of verse 21 (*shôt* and *shôdh*). In any case, the inspired writer is not to be denied a delicious irony when he puts on the lips of Job's unseeing, pompous friend a promise of security from calumny or slander. Like a stern magistrate pronouncing sentence, Eliphaz is carried away by his own masterly handling of the case, and finishes with a flourish:

>"Lo this, we have searched it, so it is;
>Hear it, and know thou it for thy good."

Always he had hankered after an authoritative pronouncement, and now his words are uttered as authoritative and final.

JOB'S TORTURE: GOD AND MAN ALIKE ESTRANGED, Chapter 6

- 6:1-7. Tasteless words! You take no sounding of my grief, nor do my own rash words give its measure.
- 8-13. May God pity me and finish me off, so frail I am!
- 14-23. Disappointment of desert travellers deceived by hopes of a watercourse and perishing because the water had dried up: such woe my friends have brought on me.
- 24-30. Let me appeal to you. Surely you see how desperate my plight is. I am hiding nothing. Please speak to my condition!

Not what his friend had perceived but what he had ignored leaves Job aghast. To what Eliphaz imagined he had perceived, conveyed as it is in dark pictures of the doom of the hardened offender against God, and presumably aimed at Job, Job will only briefly reply. In 6:28-30 he will say, "Not guilty."

There are three parts to what Job says. In 6:1-13 he says that God is oppressing him; in verses 14-30 he will say that friends are a bitter disappointment. Then in Chapter 7 he will say again that life is brief and full of misery: "I loathe my life" (7:16).

Deeply wounded by what had been said directly to him—"you are impatient . . . you are dismayed" (paraphrase of 4:5) and the rebuke in 5:2 of his heat or resentment, Job claims that he has a right to complain. No one had attempted from his words to gauge the greatness of his provocation, the greatness of his calamity (vv. 2, 3). What makes it unbearable is precisely the fact that it is God who is inflicting it ("the arrows of the Almighty are within me" and "the terrors of God," in v. 4). It is only under pressure of hunger or pain that any creature wild or tame makes a moan (v. 5). No man refuses to eat what is tasty. We complain only when that which is thrust upon us is utterly unpalatable (vv. 6, 7).

At this point the distastefulness and unendurableness of his lot comes billowing over him, and he cries in a momentary frenzy of despair, "Oh that . . . it would please God to crush me . . . [yes], cut me off!" (vv. 8, 9). Yet Job is a God-conscious man (v. 10). That is the crux of his problem: to be on good terms with God is his passionate desire. "Oh, if only God . . . God. . . ." To see how central God is to all Job's distress, we must give due weight to every mention of His name in verses 4, 8, 9, 10. Job has not disowned the words of the Holy One. Yet, exhausted as he is, Job's request is: Crush me, finish me off, for life is unbearable.

Why is it that Job so passionately craves for extinction? The answer to that question takes us to the heart of the book. It lies in the acute distress involved in "the arrows of the Almighty" and "the terrors of God" (v. 4). And it lies there not because Job has a guilty conscience but entirely because he has not. We gather from the psalmist the mental attitude of Job. In Psalm 6:1 the cry is, "rebuke me not in thine anger, neither chasten me in thy hot displeasure." Job "knows only that God afflicts; he believes that afflictions come only in anger; he feels that between his religious condition, formerly when prospered and now when stripped, there is no change. Inexplicable utterly were his sorrows." (Davidson.)

His helplessness overwhelms him: "Is my strength the strength of stones? Or is my flesh [made] of brass?" How can he wait or longer exercise patience? The wisdom of resourcefulness and fortitude to endure is quite drained away from him (vv. 11-13). His suffering truly is as measureless as the sand on all earth's shores, and this is so because "life without God's love is so empty that death is preferable" (Strahan).

Estranged from God (or so it seems), Job turns to human love. The passage from verses 14-30 begins with appeal, moves to denunciation, comes back to entreaty. The emotional tension is great, for the sense of utter loneliness and isolation is overwhelming.

The fear has visited Job's mind that he is losing faith's true hold on God. That is why he would welcome pain unsparing and death as its sequel, so that he might die without disowning the words of the Holy One (v. 10). It is this danger that makes him plead for kindness from his friends. Their sympathy might steady him if he were "forsaking the fear of the Almighty" (v. 14).

This thought is unfamiliar in Scripture on the lips of a believer, except perhaps Asaph in Psalm 73 or the strong cries of men of God in distress. Psychologically such a quick change of emotion between verse 10 and verse 14 would be very understandable. It seems unwise, following suggestions derivable from two ancient versions, here to emend the Hebrew text and read, "He who withholds kindness from a friend forsakes the fear of the Almighty" (R.S.V.). In either case the wording is unusual, but then Job was and remained unconventional. The obscurity in the Hebrew text is typical of quite a few passages in Job where the reader would strongly like a positive answer. Early translators were sometimes baffled and may be unhelpful. If Job had been as conventional as his friends there might have been no problem, but there would certainly have been no book of Job!

But if Job feels that he is in a no-man's land as regards good, his bitter disappointment now is that friends too are estranged, unfriendly. Nowhere in the book is there a more telling parable than the vivid description in verses 15 to 21 of the shame and confusion he felt through having expected sympathy from his friends and being chilled to despair. Travellers on desert wastes find in the springtime, when heat is not intense anyway, that river beds are swollen with ice and snow (professions of friendship are numerous when we are not in need). But in the fierce summer heat, travellers who turn aside to seek water where it used to be, end in consternation and despair. The parallelism of imagery and indictment is graphic, and verse 18 sums it up: "The caravans . . . go up into the waste and perish." Never was there a more biting exposure of "fair weather friends."

In scathing sarcasm Job asks them if he has embarrassed them as poor relations do by begging for money, or soliciting their support when in trouble before a court of law, or requiring ransom money to be paid for his release from bandits. Why have they gone stone-cold (vv. 22, 23)? Straight speaking, he next suggests (vv. 24-28), Let a man see where he is. Could they not focus his fault and be helpful? What should be weighed is not his words. In modern imagery we might put it this way: if his words are like molten lava, should they not picture the intense heat out of which the lava came?

He ends by claiming again, not that he is righteous in a full theological sense, but that his uprightness is not disproved by the catastrophes that have befallen him (vv. 28-30). That is the point at issue. Not to be understood and believed *here*—this is for Job the scorching, pitiless exposure to desert heat of which his parable spoke.

In all of Chapter 6 Job's loneliness is intense, and in Chapter 7 it will lead him into bitterness.

JOB SPEAKS IN ANGUISH OF SOUL, Chapter 7

7:1-10. Months of misery and wearisome nights, tossing to and fro—the flesh breaking out, infested with worms—what hope is there? And yet, to fade out in the underworld, to be nothing any more! That would be a strange conclusion as it affects God.

11-21. That being so, I ought to speak out. Life under this ceaseless inspection and persecution is loathsome. "O thou watcher of men? Why hast thou set me as a mark [to shoot at]?" Why not look away from me and let me alone? And yet . . . suppose I am laid in the dust, Thou mightest want me again and come too late!

In 6:29 the plea had been made to the friends, "Renew your investigation of my case, go over it again on other principles and presuppositions" (D). Failure of the friends to do this or to increase their sympathy, leads Job to develop his second plea, in 6:30, and declare again the sincerity of his own self-judgment.

(We have to remind ourselves that Job is battling through to what is a commonplace of the New Testament. There the apostles "glory in tribulations also," and reckon them to be a proof of sonship. In the Old Testament Job is a pioneer, painfully spelling out life's strange mixture of disaster and deserving.)

7:1-10 is reverential but full of pathos as Job describes the misery and brevity of man's life. It is toilsome (vv. 1, 2), empty of meaning, with restless tossings in the night (vv. 3, 4), and ulcers in his flesh breed worms, form a hard crust and then become running sores again (v. 5). But how brief life is—like a weaver's shuttle, a passing breeze, a vanishing cloud, and that is the end, homeless (vv. 6-10)!

7:11-21 is Job's bolder remonstrance against God.

Is Job such a formidable opponent as that monster of the waters which in early mythology had thrown the world into disorder, that God has to take repressive measures against him? Why should God pursue him in dreams, as though to undermine his morale? Sick of life, he turns in verse 17 to ask how it can be worth God's while to chase so frail and insignificant a creature as man. (This section beginning with "What is man?" is reminiscent of the trustful, grateful praise expressed with that question as theme in Ps. 8.) Instead of having God set His mind upon him (v. 17) Job requests that God will look away from him (v. 19).

This is another unfamiliar element in the Bible. Sometimes we hear of an unhealthy Christian who seems to desire God's attention almost exclusively, as though he were a "cosmic pet," but here a tormented soul complains of receiving overmuch attention from God, as though he were important enough to be God's cosmic antagonist. Chapters 9 and 10 will develop this thought of God's seemingly remorseless pursuit of him, and Job's deep distress.

The speech ends at verses 20, 21 first with a tender plea and then with a note of pathos. God's over-stringent supervision is irksome to Job (for we note in passing Job's sharp awareness of the reality of a personal God: the alternative attitude of being an atheist never occurs to him), and we remark that when stressing the sinfulness which he feels sure God can take away, he employs all the three great Hebrew words for it—sin, transgression and iniquity (vv. 20, 21). As regards Job's plea for pardon, we ought not to dismiss it as shallow or a mere piece of argumentation. In all Job's darkness, the innermost pain comes directly from the genuine experience of God that he has had. Meantime it is enough to say with A. B. Davidson, "Neither good nor evil was so fully known in the O.T. as in the New: and only when the light became clearer did the darkness grow deeper."

Intimacy with God—that alone could beget the sweet insight shown in the pathos of Job's closing words—for they are uttered to a God whom he trusts (though he appears to have been an awful nuisance to God, getting in His way, v. 20). Once Job has lain down in the dust, if God comes to look for him—He will come too late!

At 14:15 occurs once more this thought that God might seek him again. We are reminded from Job's side of Shakespeare's words:

"But I do love thee! and when I love thee not,
Chaos is come again."

BILDAD, SECOND OF THE FRIENDS, Chapter 8

8:1-7. Humble submission can win God's favor. Your children have gone (you ought to know why!) But God can give back more than you have lost.

8-19. Bygone generations garnered wisdom. The connection of sin with sorrow is clear. Plant life is full of illustrations of the slender hold on life the wicked have. So are all who forget God quickly destroyed.

20-22. Abjure your evil ways. What rapturous joy could be yours!

Less dignified, calm and conciliatory than Eliphaz, except where he relents and ends graciously, Bildad starts impatiently and argues with some heat against the stormy words of Job. These seemed to imply that God dealt unfairly with him or that God could do wrong (v. 3). In rebutting this subversive idea, Bildad is more brutal than he knows. He passes judgment on Job's children as having brought catastrophe upon themselves (v. 4). Yet he pleads with Job to seek restoration to God's favor (v. 5) and to make supplication expectantly. If this is done, Bildad assures him of a future greatly surpassing in peace and prosperity all that went before.

It is the next section, verses 8-19, which reveals the mind of Bildad. He conserves and memorizes the wisdom of bygone ages, "for we are but of yesterday and know nothing" (v. 9). All the history of the human race he counts upon as corroborating what he says. A man difficult to argue with! He has illustrations for every eventuality stored in his mind in the form of proverbs.

Papyrus, for example, shows luxuriant growth when marsh surrounds it, but how quickly it withers if the water dries up! Exactly so is the short-lived flourishing of the godless (vv. 11-13). His security is as flimsy as the spider's web, or he is like a plant in stony ground which lacks sufficient earth to nourish it (vv. 14, 16). Bildad seems more wedded to his illustrative "cautionary tales" than to close observation of the men and women who sin and suffer and need his comfort or instruction. In verses 18 and 19 Bildad's abhorrence of the wicked and his "joy" has a flavor about it which seems too much like grim satisfaction.

It is hard to conceive how the above speech could touch Job's need. This platform speaker, absorbed with the matter of his address, lacks the apt approach and appropriate action and word for each individual which was our Lord's great characteristic.

Bildad closes by reaffirming two-way reward and retribution (v. 20). This is his inflexible yard-stick, but he has hopes for Job and ends with an enticing picture (he was being as realistic as he knew how) of Job's mouth filled again with laughter. All three friends in the First Cycle of their speeches (but none do it in the Second Cycle) make similar invitation and appeal to Job (see 5:8-27; 11:13-19).

Job's Faith Is under Heavy Strain, Chapters 9 and 10

Through tempest and darkness Job will hold to the conviction that God has the answer to his problem. Increasingly, however, he is goaded by the arguments of his friends into speech that clears himself and therefore puts the blame for his appalling sufferings on God. To the minds of his friends Job, or else God, must be in the wrong: the views held in their time were such that no alternative other than this was open. Then obviously Job must be guilty, and had brought all this calamity upon himself. In the circumstances of the discussion, we as onlookers can discern that "Job has not yet calmness sufficient to see that both he and God may be righteous."

This is not to say that Job's torment arises out of a problem that is unreal. Far from it. In Chapter 9 we shall see three important truths emerge. First, we must be assured of the character of God, otherwise how continue to use the name "God," a name different from every other word in the dictionary? Unless God is light and in Him is no darkness at all, how could we worship, trust, obey? Secondly, the Book of Job is not merely concerned with the problem of suffering, but with the more inclusive subject of faith in God. Thirdly, the gropings and anguish of Job lead him to strike out this flash of light in 9:32, 33, "He is not a man as I am. . . . There is no umpire between us." "There is one God," but how bare and inadequate that truth is! It needs completion thus: "There is one God and one Mediator between God and man, the man Christ Jesus." "No man hath seen God at any time: the only-begotten Son who is in the bosom of the Father, he hath disclosed or revealed him." Job felt the acute pain of despair: it could not be dull despair but sensitive and passionate despair, just because he had glimpsed the goodness and the glory of God and therefore held on his way through nightmares of thought, facing phantoms and spectres of the mind. It is into such a wilderness of temptation that we follow him in the next two chapters.

CLIMAX OF JOB'S ANGUISH AND OF HIS AUDACITY, Chapter 9

9:1-12. "But how can a man be just before God?" Is He not Omnipotent and All-wise? Who could establish a point against Him?

13-24. "How then can I answer Him?" The perfect and the wicked alike are destroyed and overturned by Him.

25:35. "Why then do I labor in vain?" "He is not a man, as I am: there is no umpire betwixt us."

Harking back to the main question of Eliphaz, "Shall mortal man be just before God?" and to Bildad's rhetorical question, "Doth God pervert justice?" Job, even while admitting the theoretical truth of that position, suggests that God being invested with all the prerogatives of a dictator is not answerable to man. How can we be sure that we know Him? Who dare put a question to Him?

To most Christians the Allah of Islamic faith seems cold, remote, the embodiment of arbitrary will and absolute power. It is for this reason that Job's penetration to the thought of a mediator, someone nearer to man, in verses 33, 34, seems such an important flash of revelation. Like a spark struck out of the midnight of his gloomy foreboding, this inspired upsurge of longing becomes an intuition, a hint to us of the Incarnation. This will be caught up and carried farther in 16:18-21 and in 19:23-27.

Meantime what engages our attention is the intolerable darkness out of which that glowing hope was born (hardly yet a hope for Job himself). Job had reached the terminus of his thinking when he confronted the possibility that God is nothing but sheer omnipotence. The next step, in verses 13-14, is toward the contemplation of a mere juggernaut, for whom moral distinctions (vv. 22-24) are obliterated—someone arbitrary and, we are forced to conclude, irresponsible. "If it be not he, who then is it?" At this point, Job has his back to the wall—or is there any wall?

Returning to examine these first two sections of Chapter 9 we recall that Job began with the thought of a court of law, yet he treats as absurd the idea that a man could summon God to appear on equal terms, and to secure a verdict. Everything goes, in the Arab's theology, "as He wills it." Verses 4-10 give an impressive series of glances at God's power in the created universe, "uprooting the mountains, shaking the solid earth, obscuring the sun, sealing up the stars, treading on the waves" (Strahan). But this picture (it will be given a better setting when God speaks out of the whirlwind in chaps. 38-41) is exactly what the last three decades of human history have led us to describe as dictatorship. What a dictator has in his mind is unpredictable (v. 11) and he, being vested with power, is irresistible (v. 12). "Who will say unto him, 'What doest thou?' " Had even the primeval sea-monster of legend, Rahab, withstood Him?

An impartial hearing? Job carries forward this hypothesis in verses 13-24. Saddened as he had been by the thought of God as inscrutable (v. 11-"he goeth by me, and I see him not"), Job becomes embittered by this unheeding disdain. (Elihu will answer this point at 36:5.) Implacable anger and unmoralized power—that is all Job sees, power that could bludgeon or brainwash an innocent victim into pleading guilty (vv. 14-20). Such a Being—might I expect him to answer my pleading and supplication (v. 16)? I simply could not believe it!

In revulsion from this dread spectre of the mind, this unmoral Tyrant, Job plunges boldly into denunciation. He refuses to be browbeaten. (Vv. 20-22 fail to give the meaning in K.J.V.) He indicts this Adversary, for that is now the way Job conceives the one responsible for the moral disorder of the world. Going too far, Job sees injustice everywhere (v. 24)—"He covereth the faces of the judges" of the earth.

After a brief pause from his audacious speech, Job comes back to the pathos of life's brevity (vv. 25, 26) conveyed in three life-like pictures which have a strange softening effect upon Job himself. These vivid glimpses of the world he has loved— a swift-footed courier, a ship running before the wind, and a swooping eagle— almost transform his mood in favor of still being a man. Yet his despondency has one more fling in verses 27-31. (Has not some one said that the misery of being miserable is exquisite, and we like it?)

But Job's lashing tongue, which had previously said, "It is all one, therefore I say, he destroyeth the perfect and the wicked" (indiscriminately) (v. 22), now goes on to a more venomous charge: "If I wash myself with snow water, and make my hands never so clean, yet wilt thou plunge me in the ditch" (vv. 30, 31). But, as often happens, the darkest hour is just before the dawn. As Davidson well says, "Job's troubles had not overthrown but shaken and confused his trust in God." Longing for God, and a sense of life's sweetness, visit his soul like shafts of sunlight breaking through cloud. But even the wish he expresses for an arbiter or mediator (although it necessarily means far more for us who read it than it could at the moment signify for Job), for someone to lay his hand upon Job and upon God (v. 33), indicates a momentary interlude of peace. It seems more believable that God might yet take his rod away from his perplexed servant, and cease to affright him, but give him freedom to speak (vv. 34, 35).

Has there not been a welcome touch of irony in the fact that Job has used this freedom of speech amazingly well, as psalmists and prophets also do—so intimately do they know the God whom they sometimes accuse of hiding Himself (Isa. 45:15; Jer. 20:7)? Well does H. W. Robinson say of Job, "The living faith within him persisted in putting forth new shoots." Like the agonised father of Mark 9:24 Job at the same time believes and is conscious of unbelief. Like a man suffering from frostbite, on entering a house centrally heated, he is made to feel more agonising pain indoors than if he had stayed outside and been frozen to death.

In all this chapter Job has been driven by despair and a sense of wrong into violent antagonism, says Davidson, "because he and his adversary are (a) incommensurable; (b) there is no arbiter to see justice done between them; (c) the divine terror paralyzes Job, but if on equal terms he would speak and not fear, vv. 32-35." Entreaty will be the note of Chapter 10 in its middle section, but outspokenness still characterises its opening and its close.

JOB'S APPEAL TO GOD AGAINST GOD, Chapter 10

Helplessness had been the keynote of Chapter 9. Job seemed completely without refuge or resource against a grim, implacable adversary or judge (v. 3, 15). "He is wise in heart and mighty in strength. He goeth by me . . . He passeth on also, but I perceive him not. . . . He breaketh me with a tempest. . . . He will not suffer me to take my breath." Only twice in a long chapter is God's name used. Otherwise it is always "he," "he," as though unnameable. Only in verses 28 and 31 had Job said, "Thou."

But the remarkable thing is that Chapter 10 shows Job speaking throughout directly to God. Always he says, "Thou." It is prayer, all the way. Though he still may be saying bitter things, yet he is turned toward God. What he says sounds like despair, but the direction in which he is facing is the important matter and raises hope—a hope that will catch fire at 16:18-21.

Says McFadyen, "It is because God and His love are everything to Job that he cannot bear to think of Him as his enemy." Even a keener edge is given to this thought by Coleridge:
"To be wroth with one we love
Doth work like madness in the brain."

1-7. "I will say unto God, 'Do not condemn me; show me why. . . .'" The divine nature? The character of God? Art Thou human —only too human? Taking pleasure in wanton destruction of what took such pains to make, aye, or in blatant injustice (v. 3)? Hast Thou eyes of flesh, with limited perception? Are Thy days finite, driving Thee on to overhasty action? to over-eager research into my sinfulness, to inflict a penalty? But I couldn't escape Thee anyway, and besides, as Thou knowest, I am not one of the wicked.

8-13. At verse 7 Job had said, "There is none that can deliver me out of *thy hand*." Now, after a brief pause, he says, "But [it was] thy hands [that] fashioned me . . . and wilt thou bring me into dust again?"

Dwelling on what seemed his Creator's love in making and preserving him, Job appeals as to a Craftsman or Artist in God against his present plight. But at verse 13 a dark thought enters his mind, the nightmarish thought that his awful state might have been the intention hidden in God's heart when He made Job.

14-17. Job pursues the thought of God's relentless investigation, saying as it were: Suppose I have committed a minor offense, or even am downright wicked—there is no escape; even if I am innocent, my head would hang down in shame, drunken with grief. Suppose I lifted my head, Thou wouldst hunt me as a lion, varying the attack and pressing it home.

18-22. Why then was I ever born at all? Non-existence would have been best. "Let me alone, that I may take comfort a little, before I go whence I shall not return," to a land dark and chaotic.

ZOPHAR, THE THIRD FRIEND, SPEAKS, Chapter 11

Whereas a modern scholar sees in Job a "mind whose fertility no pain can destroy," his third friend treats him as Bunyan has treated the character called Talkative. We are reminded of H. W. Robinson's assessment of these three men, Job's friends: "They were not cold-hearted hypocrites; they were good and sincere men, whose chief defect was that suffering had not unlocked the door for them into the larger world of Job's thoughts." The same writer points out that Zophar "says the unkindest thing in all this debate" (11:6c).

1-6. "Should a man full of talk be justified?" If only God, the All-Wise would speak, you would see and know "that God exacteth of thee less than thine iniquity deserveth," (v. 6). Job is appallingly guilty! Zophar, alas, has marred his speech by mimicry of his wretched friend's manner of speaking (v. 4). He had, of course, been shocked.

7-12. El Shaddai, the Almighty (the name occurs 31 times in the book)—"Can you discover the deep things of God? can you reach the Almighty's range of wisdom?" (v. 7; Moffatt). The height, and depth, and length, and breadth of it surpass man's capacity to grasp. (Those four dimensions are the same that Paul will dwell on when extolling the love of Christ in Eph. 3:18.) Emphasis falls on the verbs "discover" and "reach." The familiar form of words is hallowed: "Canst thou by searching find out God?"

It is noteworthy that Zophar claims the insight into God's ways and thoughts, however transcendent they may be, that fits him to pronounce upon Job, and upon "hollow" men. The proverb he quotes in verse 12 is difficult. It seems to mean that a wild ass of a man like Ishmael (Gen. 16:12) remains untamed even when God chastens. This appears to suit Zophar's low estimate of man, but some transition towards a more hopeful view of God's ability to transform man seemed called for as a preparation for what he says in verse 13.

13-20. These eight verses show an unexpected tenderness in Zophar. There is (1) Pleading for a true conversion of heart (vv. 13-15); (2) Promise of renewal till life is clearer than the noonday, and misery altogether forgotten (vv. 16-18); and (3) Prospect of lying down with none to make him afraid, and with enhanced prestige, whereas (this is by way of warning) the wicked have no prospects at all.

Is this plea to put away iniquity and set his heart aright persuasive with Job? No, although it was a little masterpiece, of even greater beauty than the similar pictures of "returning and rest" that were painted by his friends. Job's reaction to it is depression. At 12:5 he will say, "In the thought of him that is at ease there is contempt for misfortune." No ploughshare had gone through Zophar's heart: how could his facile words minister to Job's need?

Job's Fourth Speech, Chapters 12—14

Having listened to all three of the friends, Job makes his first attempt at a real answer. First he ridicules their claim to a monopoly of wisdom. True, he says, God alone has wisdom and might on the scale of creation, but this is lordship known to creatures with feather, fur, and fin just as well.

No, says Job, stung by the devastating words of Zophar which declare that he has actually come off far better than he deserved. Retribution as the friends see it is not the principle on which the universe is run. "The secrets of wisdom" expounded by Zophar at 11:6, with retributive punishment as the main idea, rankle in Job's mind ("The perfect man is a laughing-stock," 12:4, or "Your memorable sayings are proverbs of ashes"—burnt out, no longer valid!). He therefore goes on from 12:13-25 to reaffirm his sense of the irregularities and inequalities he has observed in the moral control of the world. God (though Job avoids the name and keeps saying "he" instead), overturns moral order, He is subversive, and acts capriciously.

In Chapter 13 Job again begins impatiently, irritated by the friends as forgers of lies and physicians of no value. His aim is to get past them to God and to "reason" with Him. He declares that they have spoken unrighteously for God, that they are partial, as God Himself will confirm by rebuking them.

It is toward God that Job is hastening. After 13:20 the friends are forgotten, and Job is either pleading with God or thinking aloud in God's presence. This is so right on to 14:22.

The section of transition (13:13-19), where Job is turning from his friends to God, deserves attention if we are to discern aright the temper of his mind. At all hazards he prepares to come before God, setting his cause in order and maintaining his integrity. Two considerations should be in the reader's mind.

1. Is Job as recklessly defiant as his friends think, or is his impetuousness due to the intolerable one-sidedness of their exposition of the dogma of proportionate reward and retribution?

2. Is Job's insistent plea for liberty to come before God, praiseworthy in the full sense? Is there perhaps evidence in Job also of a defective sense of his own sinfulness? Is there humility enough in 13:23 to make it genuinely penitential? "It is one of

the aims of the book," says Davidson, "to inculcate a deeper sense of sin. It was one of the aims of Job's trial to beget this in him."

JOB'S HOPELESS PERPLEXITY OVER THE MORAL ORDER, Chapter 12

12:1-6. Job ridicules the claim to exclusive wisdom made at his expense by the friends.
7-12. Even the lower creatures recognise God's sovereign and sole control, but that does not say you have described it aright.
13-25. "With Him is strength and wisdom"—we all agree to that. But what a strange mixture of confusion shows up on earth!

Biting sarcasm marks Job's rejection of the perception shown by his friends. It is altogether too elementary. Their contempt for his misfortune inflicts a deep, envenomed wound, for Job is an Oriental in his sharp reaction to being a laughing-stock. At 19:18 we shall see how sensitive he is to the mockery of children. The might of God's hand—Job knows it only too well.

But all this humiliation to Job has proceeded while men of violence, robbers whose sword in their right hand is their god (6c marg. reading, A.S.V.) go scotfree. They provoke God and enjoy security. What has been said in verses 4-6 will be expanded from verses 13-25, but meantime verses 7-12 deserve attention.

The whole realm of animate life in earth, sea, and air is open to view, says Job, and dumb creatures and we ourselves recognise that whatsoever is done, God is the doer of it. That covers Job's afflictions too, for the life and breath of every living thing is in the hand of—Jehovah, the Lord. Israel's covenant name for God comes in here unexpectedly, more so than at 28:28, but these are the only places apart from the Prologue and closing chapters in which the name occurs.

Sovereignty? We all acknowledge it, says Job, but of what nature is it? From Lucretius to Voltaire and atheistic communism and the cultural or scientific "humanism" of the West, the statements about to be made by Job are commonplaces. Impersonal "forces" and "processes" are traced, and many follow Thomas Hardy into lighter or deeper gloom in a doctrine of determinism or dark fate. Dark as the sky was for Job, impenetrable the mystery of earth's injustices, the atheist's position was not contemplated: it was inadmissible. For a modern scientist faith in a personal God may be difficult, but Job reminds us that where there is mental conflict or even torture, the subsequent enrichment may be that much the greater.

Sovereignty in wisdom and might appears to Job unpredictable. Or is it not completely despotic? Arbitrary power, like that of an unquestioned dictator, can break down so that there is no building up again: it can imprison a man, and he has no claim for liberty (v. 14). Over the earth floods may spread, or on the contrary there may be drought (v. 15).

After these two preliminary instances from human life and inanimate nature, Job moves forward with "this fearful conception of Providence" and confines it now to the human level, first among individuals whom we would call the VIPs of the earth, and afterwards, in verses 22-25, among nations.

The biting sentence which opens the renewed attack from verse 16 indicts the government of the world as morally indiscriminate: "the deceived and the deceiver are his." God is counted responsible for what they are and do, both "the cheat and his victim," and for what "frustrates all human endeavor, and overthrows all human institutions" (Driver). Students of politics and history, and not least, observers of the world scene in the late twentieth century, would not lack illustrative material for all Job's instances of "nations misled by their statesmen into a disastrous policy" or of the overturning of "other classes of ancient lineage and secure position" (vv. 17-25, I.C.C.). On what principles does God do all this? Is it not all completely inscrutable?

Always it is the concrete individual instance of which the Hebrew Bible speaks: it does not deal in generalisations or abstractions as we of the West do. In each half verse there is a picture in Job's mind, yet he was only amplifying a previous argument with further examples. His real answer to Zophar comes later, in Chapters 13, 14.

"IF I PERISH, I PERISH" SAYS AUDACIOUS JOB, Chapter 13

13:1, 2. Job, eager to dismiss the friends from his mind, repeats his claim to understand what God is doing.

3-12. But it is to God Himself that Job desires to present his case, and he is sure God will rebuke the friends for having spoken of him like court flatterers, unrighteously. God will not approve their partiality. And who could applaud their skill?

13-19. Though it cost my life, I must press through to God and plead "Not guilty." Fear of death (in a terrific conflict) has been overcome: "I know I shall be justified" (v. 18; read A.V. or A.S.V. *marg.* not "I know that I am righteous ").

20-28. Job's two requests, on the threshold, to God are for ease from his pain, and shelter from God's terrifying majesty. Then with new confidence he would either listen or speak, ready to know the cause of God's anger. With more reverence and humility, Job now pleads not his integrity but his helplessness and frailty —a driven leaf, dry stubble.

Few chapters so resemble the Psalms at their most intense in depth and height as this one. Opening with bravado towards the friends, declaring his readiness to argue his case with God, Job's mind is a meeting place of contradictory ideas and emotions. Ready to challenge God as unrighteous to him, Job is yet sure that God will expose the dishonorable conduct of his friends and the flimsy defenses they have built (vv. 1-12), for God will not uphold unrighteousness.

Then begins a fierce inner battle between conflicting emotions, the tides flowing forward and back. A defiant assurance yields to a tremulous despair, yet when he is on the brink of death (v. 14, 15) a gleam of hope emboldens him to expect access to God, for it is strangely comforting to recall "that a godless man shall not come before Him" (v. 16). Confidence becomes established now, and quietness returns as he says, "Behold now, I have set my cause in order: I know that I shall be justified" (vv. 17-19).

"Oh that God would speak!" So the friends had said, menacingly (11:5). Job takes this up, warning them that God's appearing will not be for their comfort—"Oh that ye would altogether hold your peace" (13:5-11). Yet his own resolve to go forward to meet God suddenly leaves him weak, in awe and terror. "Behold, He will slay me; I have no hope"; nothing to wait for but certain death, *and yet he waits!* Not trust in the full sense, but "reckless tenacity"! (vv. 15, 16).

Who can expound this section or know its meaning, who but Luther in the cross-currents of longing for justification by faith and the fear that it cannot, cannot be! While the familiar translation, "Though He slay me, yet will I trust in Him" (v. 15), cannot be upheld as entirely exact or fitting the context, yet the fading out of Job's antagonism to God and his growing awareness that his weakness and frailty form a plea that God will not despise, exactly indicate the mysterious birth and growth of faith. From absorption with "my cause" (v. 18), Job advances toward a willingness to contemplate "my trangression and my sin" (v. 23). That is where faith becomes stronger. In the final section of Chapter 13:20-28, Job will acknowledge his personal, spiritual fallibility ("sins of my youth"). Because, says Davidson, he objectivizes himself here as a typical man, "like a rotten thing that consumeth," he will become ready for that glimpse of "resurrection life, when wrath shall have expended itself for sin, and the voice of God calls men from the grave to a new bodily life with Him beyond," which will form the theme of the next chapter (14:13ff.).

Yet the close of Chapter 13 still resembles the confluence of two strong streams whose waters, darker and clear, still flow along in parallel currents, neither as yet absorbing the other. It presents a more teachable Job, more ready to be shown both his sins and his sinfulness (vv. 23, 28), while continuing to ask questions and complain of being made a source of public derision, "in the stocks" (vv. 24-27). He is at the place where hopes and fear alternate, but still not immune from a further assault of despair.

The parallel is not exact between Job and Queen Esther when she resolved to approach the royal presence of Persia, and said "If I perish, I perish." Yet the hope hiding in the heart of her words is not very different from Job's breathless, deathless words.

JOB'S INSTINCTIVE FAITH IN LIFE BEYOND DEATH, Chapter 14

14:1-6. Man's fleeting life—like a flower, like a shadow.
   7-12. A tree, when felled, may sprout again, but man lieth down and riseth not.
 13-17. And yet, can that be the whole truth? If, as we know, God has a desire toward us, may He not call for us afterwards and get an answer?
 18-22. Relapse to the common view that man is merely a part of "nature," and "he passeth."

The oppressive weight of his own case and problem has been eased from Job's heart. The obsessive "I" is out of sight (except, legitimately, at v. 13), and the chapter begins impressively with the word "Man."

First man's frailty and the brevity of his life are recalled, and the essence of it (after the Incarnation we may add, and the glory of it) lies in this, that he "is born of a woman." Turning to God incredulously, Job asks, "And dost Thou open thine eyes upon such a one?"

But with mention of God's judgment at verse 3 and man's strained soul at verse 4, the request is made, "Look away from him."

Just as Job's earlier words about counsellors and kings and eloquent men being overturned in the anarchy of their time had recalled Hamlet ("the time is out of joint"), so now Job's dislike of pursuing the thought of guilt and judgment reminds us why it was that Hamlet dared not think of ending his own life—his conscience was haunted by the thought of his accountability to God afterwards. There develops in this chapter a sense of man's significance to God, even when Job is bemoaning the meaninglessness of human life. It is Strahan who points the full consequences of Christ's coming, for he takes Job's description of man at verse 20—"he passeth" and adds the overwhelming answer in the New Testament conviction that *"we have passed* out of death into life" (1 John 3:14).

"There is hope," says Job, "of a tree" and his mind dwells on shoots that come from a stump which looks dead, but the analogy between man and animate creation is thrust aside, in favor of the vanishing of water that evaporates—"man expires and where is he?" This unreadiness to accept a future life as believable must be grasped if we are to appreciate the contribution this book is to make. Job, you see, is looking for a solution to the uneven balance of pain or pleasure apportioned to men *in this earthly life*: the likelihood of a future life in which ultimate justice is done has no place in the thinking of his contemporaries, so he rejects it. Later he will come back to the thought: immortality cannot therefore be dismissed as mere wishful thinking. It is a deduction from man's fellowship with God: when God calls, having a yearning toward the work of His hands, the soul will answer Him, just as the child Samuel did. Job is fond of this thought, God calling and the soul making response (13:22; 14:15).

Job cannot go on thinking of man—of few days and full of trouble, of man lying down and rising not. He is bound to come back to his own great distress: he is bound to speak again to

God directly. In verses 13-19 the word that echoes in the ear is the word "Thou." It is out of a cluster of such communings of his soul with God (in the verses before and after it, mark the frequent occurrence of the word "Thou") that the quivering question is put: "If a man die, shall he live again?" (v. 14). Hidden in Sheol and then called forth—for God "remembered" him—once the dread day of wrath was past, Job would taste resurrection life. ("Remembering," with God, is never a mere mental state: it means that He acts, too.) It is on the verge of this hope that his mind trembles, dwelling again on God's affectionate desire for those He has created. Again, however, his mind cannot sustain this flight of hope, and he falls back at verse 16 to, "But now . . . dost thou not watch over my sin?"

This gloomier aspect continues to fill his mind till the end of his speech. Mountains fade away, rocks are displaced, earth is washed away by erosion—man's sad lot is to miss completely the awareness of his children's joys and successes or sorrows. "Thou changest his countenance and sendest him away," and still he is a sentient being. His flesh "molders in the grave" but his soul does *not* go marching on. It dimly exists in Sheol.

On this sad note Job's fourth speech and the First Cycle end.

Second Cycle of Speeches, Chapters 15–21

All through the First Cycle of speeches attention was focused on the rightness of all that God does, and the friends intended Job to recognise that suffering had come on him because of sin. Repudiating any such guilt as could bring such heavy affliction, Job had been goaded into drawing the opposite conclusion—that there is an awful lot wrong in the way God administers this world of ours.

The tumult in the mind of Job (like the troubled sea that cannot rest, in the prophet's description, Isa. 57:20, 21) led his friends to the prophet's conclusion, that there is no peace to *the wicked*. Besides, had not Job made a soul-shaking revelation of his state in the unanswered prayer, "Wherefore hidest thou thy face, and holdest me for thine enemy?" (13:24).

Along with their appeal for a penitent approach to God, each of the friends had also painted a glowing picture of the restoration, repose and riches that would accrue to him.

But now there is a change. Job had thrown out the argument in favor of ideal justice as marking all God's ways with men on earth. He had also seemed hardened in impenitence. Therefore no kindly appeal will be made to him as "an essentially pious and right-minded man," nor will glowing pictures of the consolations of God be set before him. Instead it will be the terrors of judgment here and now. All three friends will marshal their gifts of oratory to show that it is the wicked who are afflicted (since Job is afflicted, he must be wicked). Bildad and Zophar take their cue from Eliphaz, as will appear from a display of their words as they warm to their case: *The wicked man travaileth with pain all his days* (15:20), from Eliphaz; *The light of the wicked shall be put out* (18:5), from Bildad; *The triumphing of the wicked is short, and the joy of the godless but for a moment* (20:5), from Zophar. This Cycle ends with Chapter 21, the answer of Job.

THE WICKED MAN'S DARK AND HOPELESS FATE, Chapter 15

15:1-6. Eliphaz reproves Job for his bluster and blasphemy.
7-16. Was Job the earliest edition of the counsel of God? Why does he disdain the consolations of God? Are men, or angels, or the heavens clean in God's sight?
16-35. Uncontaminated truth is here (says Eliphaz); distress and anguish are ever the doom of the godless.

Deeply offended personally by Job's contemptuous attitude, the oldest man of the company (older, it seems than Job's father, v. 10) answers with sarcasm, Are you the great original of all God's handiwork? (He applies it in the realm of wisdom or insight, and not in reference to being blameless.) Why then was Job's speech as turbulent as the east wind, and so subversive of true religion? For Eliphaz, Job typifies man in revolt, irreverent, insolent, and, for the covering over of his own guilt, using the tongue of the crafty (vv. 1-10).

With the unself-conscious arrogance of pompous men, Eliphaz refers back to his own first message to Job as having offered him the consolations of God. Then he had been gentle toward Job. Now he rebukes the violence of his demeanor, his vehement speech and eyes flashing with anger. Again referring to what came to him awesomely by revelation in the night watches (4: 17-21), Eliphaz dwells on human depravity. The awesomeness of the Divine holiness (for it excels that of angels and of the sapphire or terrible crystal of heaven) is such as should restrain Job's presumptuous self-confidence. Buchanan Gray brings out the meaning of verse 16b as a description of Job as "one who deliberately soaks himself with unrighteousness . . . in great gulps, greedily like a thirsty man."

So we are watching an artist who is going to load the canvas with the darkest colors, in verses 17-35. The fate of the wicked man supplies the speaker with a congenial theme, and his other two friends likewise. The tradition they represent (vv. 17-19) is pure, uncontaminated by such alien elements of doubt as Job has introduced.

After this long preamble, at verse 20 begins a series of spine-chilling descriptions of the wicked man, travailing with pain all his days and with a sound of terrors in his ears, for he has set himself against God and cannot find rest. (The speakers see in life what they want to see: our Lord, as Gray reminds us, described a man free from all presentiments of evil, saying to his soul, "take thine ease, eat, drink, be merry.")

The series of cameos of the wicked man in verses 26-28 is illuminated by Strahan thus: "a warrior making an assault upon God, a brutish sensualist, a man so impious that he rebuilds waste cities which lie under the ban." Yet this daring impiety is pictured by Eliphaz as achieving a success that hangs by the most slender filament, and coming to a disastrous end. He may like a vine put forth grapes, but cannot ripen them, for the branch prematurely withers (vv. 32, 33). Calamity (darkness in v. 30) and flame or lightning may bring him to a violent death or reduce him to beggary (vv. 30, 31). Sterile—that is the word which Eliphaz writes over all the wicked man's endeavors, even when bribery and deceit, favorite Oriental methods, seem sure to prosper them.

Was Eliphaz reading all this off his copybook headings from ancient time? Job's grief, as he will soon declare, is not assuaged.

JOB'S REPLY: GOD IS MY ENEMY: HAVE I A FRIEND? YES! Chapter 16 and 17

It is the alternation of deep despair and soaring hope that make Job's experience like the temperature chart of a desperately fevered patient battling his way back to health. Like many a psalmist who cried from the depths, Job from above was drawn out of many waters and raised aloft (cp. Ps. 18 and 130). Chapters 16 and 17 represent the lowest plunge into despair he ever took. But it is Chapter 16 which contains the ascent from darkest dismay as in a frightful nightmare to an assurance that he has in heaven, not a grisly Adversary but a Friend who will take his part. Yet as though emotion is exhausted, there is a relapse through Chapter 17 so that it ends mournfully: "when once there is rest in the dust." As may be expected, analysis of these two chapters is more difficult than usual.

16:1-5. Monotony without matter, mouthings without mercy —such is your miserable comfort!

16:6-17. But worse still it is to be pursued and persecuted by an Antagonist on high, worse than his minions on earth. Death is closing in upon me.

16:18—17:2. But if I die, O earth, cry out over my blood (as over Abel's) as innocent. Ah, yes, earth may so cry, but *in heaven* I have a Witness. There is One on high who will vouch for me. To God I pour out tears that He will be on my side before God—and let the verdict be made known on earth to those who mock me.

17:3-9. Again I ask it: "Be surety for me with thyself," and before men who are so blind. May the issue be to establish good men to be steadfast in the paths of righteousness. Otherwise folks reckon me as obviously under God's curse.

17:10-16. Vain are your efforts to buoy me up and make me look for new life: all my cherished enterprises are altered now.

Sidetracked by the blunt speech of Eliphaz, Job loses ground for a while, and returns to his darkest thoughts of God. His descriptions of God as his "adversary" in 16:7-14 convey the impression of a warfare altogether too unequal. Says Strahan, Job's "imagination creates a series of pictures of the malign activity of an angry God which are almost unique in their tremendous realism. Behind all his sufferings he sees, as the Author of them, an implacable Foe, with terrible looks, piercing darts, and shattering missiles, persecuting him in bloodthirsty fury. With such an Antagonist it is hopeless to contend. . . . But it is his salvation that he never quite despairs."

At the beginning in verse 7 God is not named. "*He* hath made me weary. . . . *He* hath torn me in his wrath." It is familiar now on Job's lips: "*He* breaketh me with breach upon breach" (v. 14). So fertile is the morbid imagination, that from a wild beast tearing its prey with pitiless teeth, then taking him by the neck to dash him to pieces, the picture fades and emerges again as a warrior using Job for target practice with arrows that pour out on the ground his very vitals (vv. 9-13). Next a besieged city or fortress supplies the picture, with some giant storming the defenses and making breach upon breach (v. 14).

These vivid, gruesome pictures will be familiar to patients recovering in great exhaustion from a terrible illness. They are symptoms of a poisoned mind, and show that the valley of the shadow of death may be worse than death itself. Job has certainly confronted and accepted death as coming to him, and this means at the present stage a reorientation of his attitude concerning vindication. He had fought tooth and nail for a vindication here on earth. If his afflictions proved fatal, then he had no case: men would reckon that his guilt was established. But now a striking alternative visits his mind, only to be bettered by a heavenly solution that presses on its heels.

"There is no violence in my hands, and my prayer is pure," (v. 17), but if death does claim me, then "O earth," cry aloud my innocence (v. 18)! Yet immediately after he has made this appeal to the earth, Job goes one better. Not on earth but in heaven he seems to discern a mysterious intermediary or champion. "He that voucheth for me is on high" (v. 19, 21).

We have seen Job, like Browning's diver for pearls, plunge into depths which threatened to swallow him up, but each time he emerges with a pearl. Here is the pearl of his present speech— a figure dim indeed to him, but on his side. Christians naturally fill in the lineaments of the Mediator here as at 9:32, 33, adding as the last word of revelation 1 Timothy 2:5. What at the moment should impress us in the operations of the Spirit of truth within the sufferer's mind is that the contradictions in his lot, or in his discernment of God's ways, *were held together*. There were two opposites, negative and positive, brought alongside, as an electrician fixes them. The result—a flash of illumination!

The two brief passages must be brought together: 16:19-21 links with 17:3. After mention of the "witness in heaven" as one likely to clear his name, comes the petition to God, "Give now a pledge, be surety for me with thyself." Mention of a pledge, like bail in our legal vocabulary, implies that the hearing of Job's case is postponed. The thought of "striking hands" is of being surety for another person, but who can be surety with God or treat Him as an equal? Who but God can "cover" Job's case?

Not by steps in the logic but more by being caught up into heaven, as Paul would say, Job discerns a mystery. The pledge he asks for is that God will vindicate him, thus "God gives bail to God for Job, the creditor becomes the debtor's guarantee. . . .

Before he dies . . . he implores God to deposit now the pledge which will guarantee His effective vindication of Job in the future" (Peake). Truly the heart has its reasons that reason knows not of!

After this eagle glimpse of heaven—for altitude is never maintained in these flights—Job returns to the annoyances of dealing with blinded friends, in 17:4-16. Back comes also the thought of contemptuous rejection by men, "a byword of the people," "I am become one to be spit on in the face." Comment on such extreme humiliation may be postponed until Chapter 19 and Job's sixth speech, for it sounds too like the shadow of the cross to be set in any lesser context.

Job ends with remembrance of his gaunt condition, fearing lest "this" (v. 8), be a plight too harrowing for good men to assent to. And yet, of course, the righteous man will hold on his way and grow stronger and stronger. But it is toward the gloom of Sheol that Job's own thoughts are turned. Note that the "if" now thrice repeated in verses 13, 14 is not the "if" of repudiation as it will be throughout Chapter 31. Rather the thought is, Wait? Hope? No, I am now using "endearing names" of Sheol, corruption, the worm. I am "all set" for the grave. And as for my hope? Well, that is hidden in the grave. (Does this mean it has faded, or that it will yet blossom? The less startling alternative seems most in tune with the quiet anticipations of mere rest at the close of Job's other speeches.)

BILDAD'S SECOND SPEECH, Chapter 18

18:1-4. "Ask the beasts," forsooth! (12:7). "An adversary *tearing* you indeed! You keep tearing yourself! Is the earth to be turned upside down to suit *you*?

5-21. There is no escape for the wicked, but only extinction.

Coming nearer to what we call "personalities," as Eliphaz had done with Job, Bildad says it is not God that is tearing him in anger, but Job in a frenzy of his own. And as for this appeal of his to the earth (16:18), is the order of the world to become unnatural for his sake?

Well might the Saviour teach that the great art is not to win friends, but to be a friend and prove yourself a neighbor! (Luke 10:36).

But there will be no new pearl to look for in Bildad's speech: only the sore-beset Job can bring back a pearl. Yet Bildad is vigorous and warms to his task. The light of home, he well knows, has a strong human appeal, for the absence there of light spells disaster (vv. 5, 6). After further alarms that come to those who walk afield from their home, encountering only snares and traps and terrors, Bildad returns to the central sorrow of all, from verses 13-21, the frequent visit to this man's household of the king of terrors. What sorrow could be more sweeping to the Oriental or any human being than this, "he shall have neither son nor son's son among his people"?

A desolate home, the extinction of a whole family—was that not exactly what had befallen Job? Bildad is quite unsparing in his realism. Perhaps he attempts still to shock the listener into repentance by reference to the fate of Sodom when he asserts that "brimstone shall be scattered upon his habitation" (v. 15b). As later generations move in, their verdict will be the same as that of their predecessors: that the dwellings of the unrighteous are devoured by the firstborn of death, death's strongest child, and that is said to be leprosy (N.B.). Since Job's own body was disfigured by some unsightly variation of this, like elephantiasis, "Bildad's lack of delicacy in his allusions," as Strahan writes, "amount to ruthlessness." Even Job's tentative allusion to vegetation, "there is hope of a tree, cut down, that it will sprout again" was checkmated in verse 16: "his roots shall be dried up beneath."

I KNOW THAT MY REDEEMER LIVETH, Chapter 19

19:1-6. God and men are alike estranged, so why torment me any longer?
  7-12. Everything indicates that God is at variance with me.
 13:22. Kinsfolk, servants, my own wife, little children abhor me and are turned against me. I am a broken man.
 23-29. But I know that my Vindicator, my Goel, liveth. Beyond death I shall see him.

No longer resilient under the sharp words of a speaker of mere generalities, but crushed by the specific, inescapably personal items which Bildad sent like a shower of envenomed arrows, Job in consternation feels that people have broken him in pieces with words (v. 2). Reproached so continually ("ten times" in v. 3 is not a computer figure), he appeals against their harshness. Any error of his had certainly been a personal matter and not of the dimensions of his appalling desertion by God and man. Need the friends "magnify themselves," taking subtle pleasure and enlargement from the exercise of reproaching him? The plain truth was that God was responsible for the calamities: these were a clear case of injustice (vv. 1-6).

It is all wrong! But my cries go unheeded (v. 7). He hath walled up my way, shut me in, completely baffled. Who can scale these walls or find a path through the darkness (v. 8)? Truly I am like a man of position dethroned and disrobed (v. 9). The last remnants of human dignity and godliness are gone. He has left me naked to mine enemies, discredited, cast off. He has been demolishing me like a building that is unsightly, and uprooting me as a tree whose fall has no replacement, no hope. Kindled to great wrath as by a hated enemy, God sends against me troops who build siege works and invest me: what straits I am in! All these straits are of God's devising (vv. 11, 12).

Every destructive, subversive and humiliating action a man might pray to be delivered from is in Job's catalog. All through the action of God, yes God, he now is "destitute, afflicted, tormented." And if he is also forsaken by every human being, despised even by young children—"Have pity upon me, O ye my friends," for the hand of God hath touched me (v. 21). I am loathsome to my wife and you (vv. 13-19).

Smitten by God, as he confesses—*could* they relent? Could they cease to persecute him as God? This is the climax of his grief as of his entreaty. But Job saw his friends make not a sign of pity. It was then, shall we say, that fire celestial fell.

It is against this background of desperate loneliness and utter rejection by God and man that the climax of the chapter and the climax of the book are best seen. Browning said that there are two moments in the adventure of the diver for pearls—

"One when, a beggar, he prepares to plunge;
One when, a prince, he rises with his pearl."

It was after an abysmal plunge into forsakenness that Job in a sudden swirl broke surface with his pearl.

First, however, he made his final claim on future generations for a fair hearing. A written record of his case, something enduring, cut out of rock and then inlaid in metal for all time! This man who was of no reputation claimed vindication, and in a flash he knew that he had his request. Emphasising, against all that others might think or say, his own personal certainty, he cried, like a blind man who had been given sight, "But as for me I know that my redeemer liveth." Some One to clear his name at least, the "Goel" was a kinsman who restored broken fortunes, as Boaz did for Naomi and Ruth. Limiting his expectations within the sphere of his own poignant need, Job is saying and seeing far more than he knows.

Afterwards, says Job, God will arise and appear. He will come forward, following behind me, and stand as my vindicator and champion upon the dust of earth—over Job's grave. The scene is vividly before him. More is to follow. "After this my skin is destroyed, away from my flesh I shall see God; Whom I, even I, shall see and see *for me* [on my side], And mine eyes shall behold, and not as a stranger"—not estranged, but favorable to me, to my great joy.

Burdened with weight of glory, Job faints in the presence of joy unspeakable (vv. 25-27).

But he turns for a last word with his unpitying friends, his persecutors (19:22, 28). They say that in Job himself lies the cause of all that has come upon him ("the root of the matter"), but out from his own new certainty he warns them of God's sharp sword of Divine vengeance. That authentic note of Divine severity against the unmerciful sounds clearly from our Saviour's lips.

What Job has gained included vindication, a new vista, and the vision of God. All three are in Strahan's sentence: "What Job expects is not only a posthumous vindication, but his own recall to hear it and to see his Vindicator." "After his death he shall awake again to full consciousness, and shall see God. . . ." Who can state the end of that unfinished sentence?

Scholars well know the teasing textual problems in some of the crucial passages of Job. Patience is needed when, for instance, the question hangs in the balance between "in my flesh shall I see God," and "without [or "away from"] my flesh I shall see God" (v. 26). 1. It is clear that Job expects to die first. 2. He is sure that God will stand forward as his Vindicator. 3. He is confident that he himself will be there to hear this and to see God. 4. The exact condition Job will be in then is not unambiguously stated, not being the point at issue. The Hebrew preposition *min* can mean "away from" my flesh, in two senses, either "having left it behind" or "looking out from it." The question of the resurrection of the body was not meant to have an authoritative answer from this verse: so we must conclude.

Footnote to Chapter 19

The closer we come to the exceptional elements in Job's trial, the more overtones we hear. 1. The Prologue and the Dialogue are intimately interwoven. "None like him" in the Prologue is made to echo through all Job's claims for vindication, as also in many a psalm the suffering people of God cry out. The shadow of the cross, surely! 2. Of Job we have just heard in 19:21 the heartbroken plea to his friends, because "the hand of God hath touched me." Who could fail to link the thought with Isaiah 53:4: "Stricken of God and afflicted." The suffering is both vicarious and meant to bring revelation. 3. When Jesus came He said, "The Son of man must suffer many things and be rejected. . . ." Not to suffer merely, but "to be rejected." Bonhoeffer comments, "Had He only suffered, Jesus might still have been applauded as the Messiah. . . . But His rejection robs the passion of its halo of glory. It must be a passion without honor. To die on the cross means to die despised and rejected of men. Suffering and rejection are laid upon Jesus as a divine necessity, and every attempt to prevent it is the work of the devil, especially when it comes from his own disciples."

We should not detach the Book of Job from later Christian experience. For instance, Job's experience is surely lighted up by the following sentence: "To endure the cross is not a tragedy, it is the suffering which is the fruit of an exclusive allegiance to Jesus Christ." In the best sense therefore we should count Job also among the prophets. Their individual cross and Job's, too, "was a cross destined and appointed by God." This rejection, so movingly described in Chapter 19 and at such length, is part of the message of the book. After Calvary the Apostles grasped what Job groped so painfully to spell out.

ZOPHAR'S SECOND SPEECH, Chapter 20

20:1-11. A hasty man's hasty conclusion: Sinners suffer swift vengeance. Their joy is but for a moment.
12-19. Wickedness means sweetness turning the stomach sour and is a story of riches being returned to the owner.
20-29. Restless in his greed, appearing to devour everything, he will be rained upon by Divine wrath, painfully pierced through by an arrow bringing the terrors of death. Heaven and earth will conspire against him: darkness, fire and a flood of destruction will be his lot.

This final speech of Zophar is a variation on the theme which Eliphaz and Bildad have already treated, yet it is not to be dismissed as merely "another of the same." The reasons are: 1. Zophar has his own individuality, quite distinct in his two speeches. 2. It is after all three friends have spoken that Job makes his reply to them, and this time it will be particularly to Zophar. 3. Zophar shows the weakness of a nervous faith as well as its harshness. 4. Some of Zophar's sayings have the authentic ring of a prophet denouncing oppressors, e.g., verse 19. He misfires in his parables and terrifying pictures because he is not a Nathan inspired by God and Job is not David caught in sin.

Zophar's first words indicate that he may have been in two minds as he listened to Job: if so, he quickly decided in favor of the status quo and "rushed in where angels fear to tread." The reproaches of Job rankled in his mind. He preferred the soft cushions of self-approval to sincere investigation of a friend's distress, so he hastily fixed the label "Guilty" on to Job, and went on to say things that show coarseness of mind.

The superficial statement, out of his own "spirit" and "understanding," of God's swift action to checkmate sinners is contradicted in Scripture: sentence against an evil work is *not* executed always so speedily (Eccl. 8:11). This is what Job will deny, this easy, optimistic, "no problem" attitude of mind.

Indeed it is this nervousness of Zophar in his defense of God's ways that makes him an Uzzah, panicking in his action to steady the Ark. Job's, on the other side, was a deeply disturbed faith, but a living and growing faith just because of that. Part of this precious book's special message is exactly in line with the eleventh chapter of Hebrews. In that chapter the little word "not" is very meaningful: what we hope for is "not seen as yet"; we go out like Abraham "not knowing," and many pioneers of faith lived and died "not having received the promise."

Faith therefore is not a matter of formula. Luther is the one to state this: "Discipleship is not limited to what you can comprehend—it must transcend all comprehension. Plunge into the deep waters beyond your own comprehension. . . . Bewilderment is the true comprehension. . . . Behold, that is the way of the cross. You cannot find it yourself, so you must let Me lead you as though you were a blind man." This is the way God sometimes speaks, and He says "the road which is clean contrary to all that you choose or contrive or desire—that is the road you must take" (quoted by Bonhoeffer, *op. cit.*).

When Zophar, after watching the writhings and strugglings of Job, like an emperor moth breaking through an encircling cocoon, crushed down his rising trust in God, as in verse 27, that was "perhaps the most pitiless and venomous stroke" in his oration.

It is the mixture of God's truth, majestic and soul-shaking in its authority and power, with ill-conceived and grim-hearted human formulations of God's ways, that proved so crushing a burden to the spirit of Job. The Spirit of God instructs us by means of Zophar and the others not to speak unrighteously on God's behalf, and will instruct us to foster and encourage faith in others when that faith is on a battlefield, hard pressed and sometimes groaning as though in despair. Job is the grand reminder that God is watching over the little plant. He is determined to make it grow, even when believers get in His way.

The chapter repays close attention, being the last harangue from impatient Zophar. There is more of impatient, bludgeoning Zophar in all of us than we think. His thinking is vigorous (at least his utterance is) but untidy, sprawling, and recurs to the imagery of "swallowing down" and "eating," with gastric disturbances to follow. Insatiably voracious the wicked seemed to be.

JOB CLOSES THE SECOND ROUND OF SPEECHES, Chapter 21

21:1-16. Cross-examination of the three witnesses begins. What *are* the facts? The mystery of providence weighs me down (vv. 1-6) but this is what my eyes have seen: The wicked get on famously, and their happy children and grandchildren dance to the music of timbrel, harp, and pipe. When death at last comes it is easy and painless. They unashamedly left God out. Their prosperity, however, was not their own work. God gave it. Yet you deny all this.

17-26. How often does swift calamity overtake them? Ah, you say, God is reserving retribution for their children. But that is not your theory. Trouble ought to catch up with the wrong-doer himself. But why should we attempt to teach God His business? The fact is that death closes alike the sweet career of one man and the prolonged misery of another, and the difference is not just moral worth or desert. Your petty theories fall down.

27-34. All your supposed evidence, I know, converges as warning on me, but forget about me. Take in the wide human scene. Have you compared notes with far-travelled men? The truth is that the wicked man gets away before the crash, and men admire him, speak eulogies at his funeral, and he never lacks plenty to follow in his steps. Your theories are false—Job could add, faithless too.

Job has no theory, but since the world is God's world, despite all that defaces it, he is not afraid of the evidence. Suffering can make an honest man more fearless in his faith. So his opening words warn his hearers that he is taking up, in a way unwelcome to them perhaps, those last two phrases in Zophar's speech, "This is the portion of a wicked man *from God,* and the heritage *appointed* unto him *by God.*" A true account of God's rule of the world is what Job is after (Davidson). The friends may well be dismayed when Job is through, for Job himself trembles as he goes over it (v. 6).

Why is it, if God's government is just right, that the wicked enjoy such safety, happy children, music and prosperity unbroken when they live consciously in defiance or disregard of God? (vv. 7-15).

Job, of course, is not lured into the way of sinners. But like many another man from that day to this, debating with conservatives, he is troubled because they are not "concerned to be accurate." Reverting to Bildad's engaging description of the lighted lamp, the emblem of a peaceful, happy home, as being absent from the life of the wicked (18:5, 6), Job asks, as it were, not for a statement of poetic justice but for statistics. "How often?" Phrasemaking about stubble and chaff in the wind, so in God's anger they are carried away, is not factual enough for a man sensitized by suffering.

It is the clarity and penetration of Job's mind in this chapter that arrests us. Like a skilled advocate he has reserved till all three friends have spoken, his summing up and answer to their arguments. What he does, as Peake says, is to pulverise them.

"Anticipating an objection the friends may make," that punishment is reserved for the sinner's children, Job disallows it as not being in harmony with their own theory (v. 19). "Let God recompense it unto the sinner himself, that he may know it." By their own statements and on their principles, if this life on earth is all, retribution ought to be contemporary. A hardened sinner might be callous about the consequences of sin to his own family afterwards. (How absurd, interjects Job, to suppose that we need to take God along with us in these steps of the argument, as though we can help Him to grasp things! v. 22). But contemporaneous punishment is not the last word for Job at all, just as for Job death is no longer the last word. The latter point is meantime deferred. It can wait, since Job himself has had a vision of a Kinsman Redeemer who will stand on his grave and appear to him beyond death.

It is to death as the assumed end, death coming indiscriminately to the man "wholly at ease" and to the man dying in bitterness of soul, that Job comes back (vv. 23-34). Travelled men, with wide experience, confirm the view that death is often serene and almost a triumph of reputation for the wicked, at the time and afterwards.

As far as his friends' doctrine is concerned, it holds no comfort, no light. Job is no mere nihilist. His disordered spirit is more calm now. A man who walked in darkness has begun to see a great light.

The Third Cycle of Speeches, Chapters 22–31

What a long way Job has come between Chapter 3 with its torrent of passionate despair and distaste for life and the keenly logical examination in Chapter 21 of the theology of his friends —he, moreover, looking beyond the grave, whereas they still insist that death ends all! Job, however, is still subject to reactions of despondency in the chapters before us, notably 23. Eliphaz reminds us of the fascinating projection of character and mentality—the book's dramatic quality—when his third speech shows him intemperate in speech, grossly unjust in accusation, and finally ending (as his first speech had done) with entreaty and a glowing picture of Job's prospects at God's hand.

The structure of the Third Cycle is altered. Eliphaz contributes one chapter, 22, Job speaks for two, then Bildad in chapter 25 speaks only five verses, and thereafter Chapters 26-31 are attributed to Job.

Three features of the content of Job's speeches ought to be noted: 1. The three last chapters form a climactic closing speech of pathos and power. In 29 he describes his happy past, in 30 the lamentable present, full of rejection and dishonor, while in 31 he gathers up all his energies in a passionate repudiation of guilt, claiming on oath to be cleared of all charges. This "Oath of Clearing" coupled with Chapter 29 gives a fascinating description of the character and conduct of a man of God—the basic ethics of the Old Testament. 2. Just as Job's closing speech will lead on to the intervention of God out of the whirlwind, so there are sections beforehand which project or suggest features that will come later. The panorama of creation in Chapters 38-41 is prepared for by Chapter 28 as also by 26:5-14. Some scholars question the likelihood of its originally belonging where it stands. Thankfully we welcome it. Job's range of interest was never narrow, nor his mind warped and subjective. The artistic fitness of this prelude (following 26:5-14), to the symphony of all creation when God at last speaks, encourages us to appreciate its intrinsic qualities. It was not by accident that it was incorporated. 3. Chapters 24-27 apportion little to Bildad and nothing to Zophar. Yet portions of Job's speeches sound strange on his lips. Attentive students are grateful to scholars who have wrestled with unusual intricacies of text and grammar here. Conjectural reconstructions are offered by many. Until a perfect manuscript is discovered, we are happy to listen to Job as the author of 26:5-14 or else *reciting* it and other passages.

ELIPHAZ'S UNFOUNDED CHARGES AND UNFALTERING APPEAL, Chapter 22

22:1-4. God is too lofty for man to put Him in debt by being good. Goodness in you would not get you punished.
   5-11. You are charged with the arrogant harshness of the mighty man toward the poor, the thirsty and hungry, the widow and the fatherless. Pitiless, you receive no pity.
  12-20. Flood and fire long ago swept away the defiant, wicked men you have described and seem to make your model.
  21-30. "Acquaint now thyself with Him and be at peace."

An astonishing speech. It begins with a faceless God, moves forward into libelous charges with no shred of evidence or second witness to sustain them, classes Job with the godless men of Noah's time or Sodom, and then closes with a peal of bells to entice home and welcome there a returning prodigal.

The assumption which gave a fatal twist to the thinking of the friends was that Job was being *punished.* The thought that suffering can be vicarious had not become known, still less the crowning truth of vicarious suffering that discloses to us the heart of God. Eliphaz talks like a man without knowledge as the chapter opens, for his attempt to prove Divine impartiality in judgment starts off by saying that man's conduct is a matter of indifference to Him: He is "above all that"! How deeply "involved" God really is, Moses had to be shown (Exod. 3:7-10), and the prophets were told (Hos. 2:14; 6:4; 11:8; Isa. 63:9; Ezek. 6:9) and Gethsemane fully declared.

"Is not thy wickedness great?" coming from the lips of Eliphaz made someone remark that one aim of this book is to show how God has sometimes to be defended from His friends! Courteous men are discourteous when a wrong theology distorts them, or a feeling of insecurity in their faith makes them cruel. Blessing and cursing, sweet water and bitter—out of the same mouth! How can it be? These specific charges against Job made by Eliphaz highlight the warning of James about the tongue, and also bid us keep our heart with all diligence. It is a sin to surmise wrong things of others. Not "snares . . . sudden fear . . . darkness . . . abundance of waters" but the arguments and suspicions of friends tried Job most severely. "Is not God in the height of heaven?" introduces at verse 12 the question whether Job considers God so far removed that He does not see all that men do. "The old way which wicked men have trodden" (v. 15), refers to the unashamed scoffers in Noah's day, and God's action is evidence of God's government, evidence that makes the righteous glad. In adducing such an instance, and also the reference in verse 20 to fire over Sodom, Eliphaz quotes Job's words from 21:14 as though Job approved of this attitude, which is quite contrary to Job's intention.

But Eliphaz in the last part of his final speech moves back into the eager exhortation and glowing promise that marked the peroration of his first speech in 5:8-11, 17-27. "Acquaint now thyself with him and be at peace" introduces a passage of surpassing beauty and truth. A close examination of all items included will furnish instruction for evangelists concerned to be sure about the characteristics of truly Biblical evangelism. "Receive the law from His mouth"; "lay thou thy treasure in the dust"; "the Almighty shall be thy treasure"; "delight thyself in the Almighty"; "lift up thy face unto God"; "pay thy vows"; each item plus the moral authority and spiritual resilience and widespread benefit to others of true reconciliation with God unfolded from 28-30, supply a program for the Christian life which could hardly be improved. It is spiritual and ethical, it covers conversion and character and conduct, and it is as God-centred as Psalm 73:25, 26. It is healthy-minded, mature, compassionate, social in its outreach.

And, strange to say, this man who could preach so well was

wrong-headed, twisted in his sympathies, and came under the rebuke of God (see 42:7-9). We all seem to *know* much better than we *do*.

JOB'S YEARNING TO GET THROUGH TO GOD, Chapter 23

23:1-9. It is God my soul craves for, Him I must find, to Him at His tribunal that my cause should come—"Oh that I knew where I might find him!"

10-17. My way is known to God, for I have made His way my way. Why then does He elude me and refuse to vindicate me, and leave me terrified even when I am confident?

"When He hath tried me, I shall come forth as gold." This confession of his soul's deepest faith is a fresh affirmation of his conviction that God is righteous and is about to vindicate Job as a man whom He approves. The truth about God and about Job forms one globe.

At this point we must go back to the Prologue and recall God's verdict about Job as a man blameless and upright. We shall get things wrong unless we grasp the fact that the very testimony God had borne to Satan in heaven (hidden from Job's eyes as it is) about Job's single-minded devotion to God and His cause is exactly what Job is claiming that God should proclaim on earth. But God is silent. Job is wrongfully accused. God is just (such is Job's basic faith) but why is God so unconcerned about appearances? God appears to be dead-set against intervening on His servant's behalf (vv. 13, 14). That is why the chapter ends with Job full of fears, his heart faint. The meaninglessness of his great calamity is what overwhelms him.

Christians have the advantage over Job because they have learned that trials *refine* our faith. Gold is purified by passing through the fire. But verse 10 had a different meaning for Job. "When He hath tried me," in Job's thought meant that the Heavenly Examiner would pronounce in his favor: "This man is not base metal, not alloy—he is gold!" Declaration and vindication of his soul's quality—a Heavenly Assize and the Judge pronouncing Job innocent—that is what the whole argument of the book is about.

Examine the chapter from the beginning with this clue. Unable to toe the party line of his friends, Job still admits to being rebellious, still complains that his groaning does not match his unfathomable grief. It is here that the pent-up, passionate longing for direct access to God finds expression: "Oh that I knew where I might find him." That first half of the chapter echoes to two words and two only: they are "him" and "me." Like the Song of Songs, it flutters with the fear of losing Him who is the soul's all-in-all. There are two strands woven into and around this central hunger for God Himself. 1. There is confident expectation, as in verse 6. "Would he contend with me in the greatness of his power?" Here the *Nay* is emphatic. The remainder of verse 6 and all of verse 7 are hopeful of God's readiness to listen, and to pronounce the right verdict. 2. The soul's search for God seems baffled. All four times the dismal hide-and-seek gives the same kind of fourfold melancholy report that the four messengers of catastrophe brought to Job. Listen: "He is not there . . . . I cannot perceive Him. . . . I cannot behold Him. . . . I cannot see Him" (vv. 8, 9).

Mystics have explored these regions of seeming forsakenness. "The dark night of the soul" was known to Job, hence the great value of the book. "Why hast thou forsaken me?" was the cry from the lips of Psalmists which our Redeemer took upon His own lips. It is not the complete answer, but part of the answer Job already grasped, and it was this: Keep on seeking Him I must: I can do no other. Another aspect of the same truth is: "Thou couldst not seek me at all, unless thou hadst already found me."

The latter half of the chapter begins bravely at verse 10, and begins by affirming God's approval of Job's "way" as meaning complete surrender. Job claims that "the way that I take" is "his way" (vv. 11, 12). Job, let us remember, is not the Everyman whom Paul is showing up to the Romans as a sinner. Job is not the typical man of the world, but the typical "servant of the Lord." Job is the "true-hearted, whole-hearted" man who like an apostle knows nothing against himself (Acts 23:1; 24:16), but is elected for suffering (Acts 9:16). Verses 11, 12 read *almost* as though the New Covenant of Jeremiah 31:33 is already true in Job's case, so greatly does he cleave to God's way and His words. "Almost," for Job is agitated, troubled, terrified, fearing that God is yet arbitrary, despotic, unpredictable (vv. 13, 14). In verse 17 "darkness" is the word Job used to describe all that had befallen him. Using it twice, he closes the first part of his speech in "encircling gloom."

Reading over this chapter again, the Christian is amazed to realise how much richer its message is for us, after Job pioneered that bleak, lonely stretch of country. "He knoweth the way that

I take" in its primary meaning held far less of comfort and many-sided assurance for Job than it now does for us. So much of fuller revelation has come our way since that ancient time; best of all a full redemption has been wrought, and the true light now shineth! No verse of Scripture can mean less to us than it did to those to whom it first came. If we fall short of the full comfort of the Scriptures, may it not be because we are not "poor . . . mourners . . . hungry and thirsting," passionately single-minded in our seeking after God, as were Job and the Prophets and Psalmists?

SURVEY OF THE WORLD'S OPPRESSIONS, WOES AND PAINS, Chapter 24

24:1-12. Why does God not appoint days of judgment and keep wickedness under control?
   13-17. Why should men who hate the light enjoy such freedom to exploit the darkness?
   18-25. Who can disprove me when I say that not Statement A but Statement B represents the actual situation?

This strange chapter has problems of text and transmission for the scholar, but sounds like a clarion call to the best kind of patriotism and the holy social concern which is at the heart of God and the godliest men and women. Translation is a teasing problem for the Hebrew scholar at numerous points, but the plain reader is all too sure that these loaded verses summon us to translate them *into action!* An immediate answer to the second section, with its topsy-turvy night-life, is supplied in Isaiah 58:10, which provides both a field of action and a promised end to darkness or obscurity in the soul.

Job was no mere introvert. The whole world's need was an urgent question for him, as 9:24 reminds us, "The earth is given into the hand of the wicked." In Chapter 12 the confusion and anarchy of this world was boldly confronted. Job is no spiritual aesthete or egotist, exclusively concerned with his own inner condition. He wants to see God's righteous, holy will done on earth as it is done in heaven.

First therefore Job decries lawlessness: the removing of landmarks (solemnly forbidden under a curse in Deut. 27:17), the driving away or misappropriation of an entire flock of sheep, or highhanded robbery of the lone ass or ox which a widow and orphan might possess. Then at verses 5-8 comes a description of vagrants or gangs in communes or victims of forced labor, miserable victims of organised greed or power, unhoused, ill-fed, hardly clothed. Exploitation! But slavery too, by the snatching from its mother's breast of a fatherless child, for they seek their miserable repayment of a trivial debt by selling the defenceless child. And after this picture from rural areas, Job adds: "out of the populous city men groan." And the comment is this: God pays no attention.

In addition to those violent wrong-doers who flout the law, there are the night-hawks, who do their nefarious work under cover of darkness: murderers, thieves, adulterers (vv. 13-17). What an extensive class of criminals operating in the night would need to be described by a Job of the late twentieth century!

A puzzling section lies before us. Verses 18-21 give one theory, the optimistic one favored by Bildad and the friends. In verses 22-24 we seem to have Job's statement of the contrary position, namely that God preserveth the (arrogant) mighty, restores him when he seemed beyond recovery, "giveth them to be in security." And then with no pain, the wicked lie down and die, after attaining the ripeness of the tops of the ears of corn.

The earlier picture of the swift destruction of evil men, where even the womb that bore the sinner easily forgets him and the worm feeds sweetly on him—Job does not see it that way. Not swift oblivion, but prolonged immunity from trouble, seems the portion of the wicked. If Job could overhear a later psalmist inditing Psalm 94, how his heart would be warmed! "He that planted the ear, shall he not hear? He that formed the eye, shall he not see?"

THE LAST SPEECH OF BILDAD, Chapter 25

The awe-inspiring sovereignty of God (Strahan's rendering of "dominion and fear") is Bildad's theme. Job will carry forward in 26:5-14 our contemplation of the Divine majesty and triumph. The triumph which Bildad refers to, "He maketh peace in his high places," was over disaffection in heaven ("He judgeth those that are high," in 21:22; cp. Isa. 24:21). In 26:12, 13 more will be said, including the mention of Rahab, first brought before us at 9:13. Rahab was the chaos monster described in Isaiah 51:9 as cut in pieces and pierced (cp. leviathan in Job 3:8; Isa. 27:1). Mysterious references like these show how strong was the tradition of primeval strife, and the imagery is colored by popular imaginings about Tiamat, perhaps. What Bildad is concerned to press home on Job's mind is the reverence due from us on earth to One who is undisputed Lord in highest heaven.

God's triumph as yet is linked with His armies innumerable, and with His light, for God's enemies are powers of darkness which flee from the light (v. 3). But the words "He maketh peace," followed two verses later by the question, "How then can man be just before God?" inevitably recall to us the New Testament revelation of how peace was made—by the blood of Christ's cross. Armies of God have their necessary place still, but Bildad compels us to recall vicarious suffering such as Job's, for it is that "mystery" not yet disclosed to the friends but gradually, dimly becoming discerned by Job. (Here by the way is an additional reason for reckoning Job to be the fitting speaker of 26:14, for that superb statement could only be attributed to Bildad by an excess of irony.)

God in His greatness—this is Bildad's subject, but not that alone. At the opposite pole is man (v. 6). To him no dignity at all is ascribed. Neither moon nor stars are clean in God's sight, nor the angels, as Eliphaz had shown (4:18). Man therefore and the son of man? Two different words for a *worm* are all that the speaker can think of!

Well, if that and only that is the preacher's business, he is a mistaken visionary and a deluded moralist. No wonder Job asks him what is the source of his inspiration (see 26:4).

THE AWESOME OUTSKIRTS OF GOD'S WAYS, Chapter 26

26:1-4. How helpful to the weary, how instructive to the ignorant are your words! Whence came your inspiration?

5-14. In the depths and in the height, God transcends all our ideas of greatness and power. How fragmentary is our knowledge!

It is unusual for Job to address one speaker only amongst the friends, but "thou" is used all through verses 2-4. Sarcasm may seem excessive if to Bildad alone, and after so short a speech. On the other hand severity in judging people for what they have *not* done is a clear Biblical principle (Matt. 25:45). Besides, how bleak and bare of help that conquering God of Bildad's theology had seemed, and how chilling was the estimate of man which went with it. A man confessedly impotent (v. 2), would have welcomed strengthening: surely such a man invites it. What a misuse of words, a misdirection of "Spirit," Bildad's speech had been!

The awe-inspiring sovereignty of God is now the subject again, but in a strain not usual with Job. Bildad began in the height of heaven: Job continues, but first in the underworld (v. 5). For "the deceased tremble," since Rephaim is the word used, Strahan translates, "the giants writhe in pain" (Deut. 2:11, 20). The thought is of God's irresistible power, but next God's unimpeachable knowledge is shown, for Sheol and the Abyss (Abaddon, cp. Rev. 9:11) are uncovered before His eyes (v. 6). The thought, unexpected from Job's lips but perhaps coming back to memory and being recited on the spur of the moment, is the same as that expressed in Hebrews 4:13, "All things are naked and laid open before the eyes of Him with whom we have to do."

Verse 7 mentions empty space (to us of the "space age"!) and tells how God "hangeth the world upon nothing." This impressive thought has value first for itself, of course, but prompts also a reminder of the poetic and dramatic development of this book, moving as it is toward the Divine intervention, when God will direct attention to His glory in the vastness and intricacy of the world He has made (chap. 38ff.).

Clouds next excite wonder (v. 8). How can they carry such weight of water? As a child asks how a sponge, so full of holes, carries water! We speak of a cloudburst: what seems to impress Job is that the rain comes normally in gentle showers, not with destructive fury. Next the clouds are mentioned as hiding God's throne from us, but they are never to be conceived as hiding us from God's sight. It was with God's full knowledge of the underworld that Job started! (vv. 10-13). The great dome of heaven, and the horizon, and "the confines of light and darkness"—what thoughts these stir in astronomers and seamen! Nowadays the international dateline in mid-Pacific would be just one of the modern amplifications of verses 10, 11. "The pillars of heaven tremble" (v. 11), may well convey that sense of overturning of mountains that is mentioned in Psalm 46:2, 3, while the "rebuke" of God reminds us of the thunder of His voice in Psalm 29. Waters may roar and be troubled, but God is in control of them and of infernal powers. Verse 13a is as eloquent as any of these majestic exhibitions of power, for in a context of storm it quietly says that by the Spirit or wind of God the heavens suddenly become fair and clear. Who has not marvelled at such sudden calm after tempest!

The conclusion of the whole matter, however—is it worship? Or is it skepticism? "Lo, these are but the outskirts of His ways: and how small a whisper do we hear of Him!" Says Davidson, "The nervous brevity and sublimity of these words are unsurpassable."

We may well picture Job as waiting. Knowing the end of the story we also know that God was waiting. God the Lord was waiting to be gracious, and Job was heir to beatitude because he was waiting for God (Isa. 30:18).

JOB IS MOVING TOWARD HIS FINAL DEFENSE AND OATH, Chapter 27

27:1-6. As God liveth, I re-affirm my innocence. This is "the tragedy of integrity." It is God who must do right by me.

7-10. Those who denounce me deserve the fate of the wicked: the wicked have no hope, no assurance in trouble, no delight in God, no solace in death. (Job reckons himself to have all these, despite appearances; hope beyond death, chap. 19).

11, 12. Let me interpret God's dealings to you ("the hand of God"). Yet you have seen it all, if only you had eyes to see.

13-23. The oppressor—sword, famine and pestilence destroy his children (vv. 13-15), his gains turn to nothing (vv. 16-19), he will be harried by terror and trouble (vv. 20-23).

The startling words that open Job's speech take an oath by the living God and then charge the living God with wronging Job, with being unrighteous (like the unjust judge of Luke 18:2-4, paying no heed). Always Job is a theist: his thinking is never impersonal, so he daringly adds, "the Almighty who hath vexed my soul," making it bitter. Yet his daring is not defiance. Missionaries have known people who really trusted them yet in their manner of speech appeared insolent, but there was no misunderstanding. Job is not sulking. He is transparent. There is living flame in him, not acrid smoke. He therefore is not unmanned, does not succumb. We marvel. Under so prolonged and intense a strain, he still saw things straight. Verse 3 must mean the same secret as is given in Psalm 63:8, "My soul followeth hard after thee: thy right hand upholdeth me."

At verse 7 we begin to wonder if we are grasping the meaning aright: Job was not vindictive, as 31:29, 30 emphatically show, but how are we to weave verse 7 in with the compassion for the hopeless wicked man which breathes through verses 8-10?

There appears to be something missing from the original text, or is something dislocated? At verse 11 Job undertakes to expound what suffering, or else the blindness of his friends, has taught him about the hand of God, but is the passage that follows in verses 13-23 the expected or suitable sequel? He has heard all that *ad nauseam* from his friends: could it be that his repetition of it all back to them has a purpose to serve? It is a sorrowful recital. Is the point of it all that Job can say it without blushing: *he* is not the man?

Job's clear conscience may well be the point at issue if the recital of calamities befalling a wicked man's children are now treated by him without turning a hair, in verses 13-15. Eliphaz had actually spoken of Job as an oppressor (27:13; cp. 22:6, 8). Sword and famine are mentioned in verse 14 as the instruments of death, and the third commonest scourge known to the Semites, namely pestilence, is the subject in verse 15. Pestilence causes rapid decomposition, so that death itself may be said to do the burying. Added to this horror came, as another inevitable indignity, the absence of mourning. "No lamentation" seemed to be the lot of Job's ten children, and no burying appears to have been needed. With equanimity Job seems capable of regarding their death in greater quietness at the moment, for we should recall that the discussion has presumably reached a third day, or at least a second ("even today is my complaint rebellious," 23:2).

After the death of persons, next in the catalog of a man's fortunes comes his property. In 16-19 the familiar theme treated is the deceiving hopes raised by possessions. The moth is the most ephemeral of creatures, and a booth was a structure hastily erected to supply a watchman's temporary need at night. A startling statement, compared by Davidson to the brilliantly vivid paradox in 2 Kings 19:35, falls from Job's lips about the wicked-rich man in verse 19b. Who but Job, who had longed for this very fate or blessing, could have conceived it? "He openeth his eyes—and he is not" (there)! Sudden destruction? Almost too good to be true? We hardly dare press the point, however, for the Job we now are listening to is no longer the Job of Chapter 3. There is still something about death: it is mysterious; there is more to it than mere vanishing.

"Such dreams may come," said Hamlet of death or after-death.

Terrors overtake the wicked man, a tempest, the east wind, and it sweepeth him out of his place. There is something so undefined about death! That is what leaves it such an infinite mystery. The detestation of the people who survive the wicked-rich man is shown by their clapping of their hands and hissing. Job at least had looked all that in the face—the unpopularity too (see chap. 30).

INTERLUDE: WISDOM IS MAN'S QUEST, GOD'S GIFT, Chapter 28

28:1-11. Man shows great skill in discovering the place where treasures are found.
12-22. But neither the place nor the price of Wisdom is known.
23-28. God—thrice over it takes four verbs to convey the knowledge and operation of God—God has brought the secret of Wisdom within man's reach. Here it is!

In this chapter controversy is stilled. After the varied enterprises of men have been reviewed—with a glance toward the loftiest birds and the proudest of wild beasts—mention is made of the undiscovered treasure, Wisdom. The main question, in parallelism, is twice put, at verses 12 and 20. "But where shall wisdom be found? And where is the place of understanding?" Then at the close comes the majestic statement made from the lips of God.

In this interlude we are being shown the pattern which the Book of Job will follow. It will be God who speaks at the end, and what had been unattainable is made Job's possession: in this case, discernment of God's plan and purpose, peace with God, and a happy acquiescence in God's ways. Wisdom is more than insight to Job, it would mean reconciliation, "and we cannot be reconciled to God and be at enmity with what He appoints" (Oman).

Wisdom, however, within this chapter hardly attains to these stately dimensions, nor to what Paul would write of it to Corinth (I Cor. 1:23, 24). It had not been such a hidden wisdom in Job's experience, as the opening sentence of the book had stated. Its inaccessibility and man's failure to attain to what he most passionately is in search of—that is what Job examines. The fact that Job had not found the heart-rest he sought for will become evident in 29:1.

Silver, gold, iron and copper, and the vivid description of mining operations, occupy the first part of the poem. The thick darkness below ground, with corn growing up above, and men precariously hanging to explore seams of precious metal—all this mysterious activity suggests more than actual words express. It would be difficult to maintain that Job is a book of pessimism when such appreciation of the pursuits of mankind is shown, and still more when earlier and later evidence of pleasure in natural phenomena, the work of God's hands, is so many-sided. A strange dignity invests human life, or why should language be so exquisitely wedded to a description of it? "That path no bird of prey knoweth, neither hath the falcon's eye seen it"—then why bother to assess it, unless it has significance and everlastingness? At verse 9 we might pause and recall that in 1965 a road was opened, tunneled below Mont Blanc. The conclusion cannot be that man is not going anywhere in particular! If it can be said of man, the seeker for earth's costliest gems, that "his eye seeth every precious thing," how much truer must it be that every self-denial, every difficult venture of faith or act of obedience, is marked by God and will have eternity for its full harvest. "The thing that is hid bringeth he forth to light"—every sentence is like this one, loaded with higher meaning than is exhausted in human endeavor, or in humanism.

"Where? Where?" this is the refrain through verses 12-22. All that kindles the imagination is gathered between the gold of Ophir and the topaz of Ethiopia, sapphires and rubies. Price? That is too commercial a word. It is something "not of this world." "The deep saith, 'It is not in me', and the sea saith, 'It is not with me!'" Wisdom is "hid from the eyes of all living." "Destruction and Death say, 'We have heard a rumor thereof with our ears.'"

With the emphatic word coming first, the third section opens: "*God* understandeth the way thereof. . . . He knoweth. . . . He looketh. . . . and seeth" (v. 23). The wind is mentioned and God can weigh it; the waters to Him are not infinite. Rain falls not by chance but at His will, and the lightning cleaves the path that He ordained. Nothing is haphazard. But what God saw and declared and established and searched out is a means of communication with man, a bridge to fellowship. "To walk humbly with God," as Micah will re-phrase it, and to hate every false way, as a meditative psalmist will express his soul's choice—this is Wisdom. Here is the chapter's climax, at its close.

Richer than this chapter will be the conclusion of Job's

troubled search, for at the end it will be a *Self*-disclosure, a manifestation of *God*. Then Job will say, "Now mine eye seeth *Thee*."

Job's Final Speech: His Summing Up, Chapters 29-31

These three chapters strictly fall outside the Discussion with the Friends, for they form a soliloquy. That soliloquy, of course, goes on in God's presence, and Job can turn from saying, "He," to say, "Thou" (30:19-23). With Job, prayer is a necessity. He could almost have written Psalm 139, so strong was his sense of God's encompassing presence in former days (cp. also 31:4).

Chapters 29-31 can be extracted from the movement back and forth in controversy. They have intrinsic worth which ought to bring them into frequent use with Christians. If I Corinthians 13 deserves frequent perusal ("read it daily for a month," was the counsel of a wise spiritual guide), then Job's review of his former way of life in Chapter 29 and his final self-examination before his Judge in Chapter 31 demand to be employed as an ethical check-up by us all, and often. Influential men, executives, preachers and teachers and parents, all should look in this mirror regularly. No more impressive flesh-and-blood "bill of rights" was ever made out for others until the Saviour spoke. Chapter 31 is not only the Old Testament's best declaration of ethical standards. Like the New Testament it gives God's law not as a code, but warm, living, and persuasive because it has been lived out.

Chapter 29 is Job's nostalgic review of bygone days, so blissful. Chapter 30 is his description of the appalling contrast he sees in the present, woeful beyond words. In Chapter 31 he braces himself for judgment because he has first cross-examined and judged himself. (A preacher once said he had decided to have his "Judgment day" *now!*)

A fascinating Bible study for a group can be made from these chapters. Keywords are "in the months of old" for Chapter 29, "but now" for Chapter 30 (with "and now" at vv. 9, 16), while "If" and "then" recur all through Chapter 31 as Job argues point by point. Job accepts the consequences mentioned by "then" "if" he has fallen down on any claim of being clear of guilt. Another study takes in outward offenses and inward attitudes, or open and secret faults, in Chapter 31, for this realm of desire and imagining, and the failure to do active good, were specially brought out in the Sermon on the Mount. The Book of Job is not going to be neglected. May many Bibles fall open at Chapter 31 through frequent handling before this Mirror of Integrity!

REMEMBERING HAPPIER DAYS, Chapter 29

29:1-6. Oh, that I were as in the months of old. Then God was my watchful Friend, the Fount of every blessing, and my children were about me. What bounty I enjoyed! Then the Almighty was with me. Ah, then!

7-10. Young men and old, both princes and nobles respectfully marked my coming, rose up and stood, or fell silent.

11-17. Such reverence arose from affectionate regard for my works of mercy to the needy, of championing the cause of the helpless, and being available to help the blind and the lame, and those without hope of redress from the unrighteous.

18-20. It seemed as though serenity and security would be unbroken, and I would die in my nest. Freshness without a hint of decay!

21-25. Yes, to be trusted like that, to be honored as making life sweeter and stronger and surer—to be held in esteem as benefactor to many—it seems incredible!

Generalities are a poor substitute for the fulness of detail in Job's warm and glowing picture of the past. The one shadow or chill wind occurs in verse 5, with the clause, "When the Almighty *was* yet with me." For this reminds him of departed joys. God was then the source and secret of all his delight at home and his influential place in community life. Life for Job had not been merely rural, for he was a city counsellor, taking his seat at the city gate. Even the rocks seemed to yield olive oil for him, and scarcity was unimagined. Milk was more plentiful than water which is sprinkled to lay the dust (a hyperbole).

The prestige he had enjoyed appears too wonderful to be believed, yet it was the natural outflow from unstrained and unselfconscious concern for others. Both doing justly and loving mercy were the spontaneous expression of his humble and happy walk with God (cp. Micah 6:8). The acceptance of his counsel, the appreciation of his action for the public welfare, the personal good-will to him, astonish Job in the retrospect, so that his modesty is undimmed. If ever there was a genuine portrait of a good man, this is it. The fragrance still on it proves that it was the direct and natural growth from unaffected and healthy piety.

JOB'S SORROWFUL REVIEW OF THE PRESENT, Chapter 30

30:1-8. *But now* I am held in contempt by the dregs of humanity.
9-15. *And now* not honors but indignities are heaped upon me.
16-23. *And now* the reversal of my fortunes is most acute where my joy was greatest: God's silence, God's hostility (here Job turns and speaks to God) leave me exhausted, despondent, gnawed by pain.
24-31. Unpitied, I recall how pity moved my heart. Mourning, I find jackals and ostriches my nearest companions. My blackened flesh rots and falls off; my bones are burned with fever. Music and joy are turned to weeping.

Bitterly conscious of the extreme contradiction which his present fate exhibits after his glowing picture of esteem, influence and honor once enjoyed, Job descends to the lowest abyss of humiliation. So extreme is his revulsion that he gives utterance to what the true Job would never have voiced: a disdain for some human beings as sub-human. Some commentators reckon the first eight verses an intrusion brought into the text from a copyist's marginal notes, but they seem psychologically convincing in this "sickness unto death," especially when self-approval may have exalted him overmuch. Creatures "driven forth from the midst of men . . . in holes of the earth and of the rocks" (vv. 5, 6), serve only to accentuate the abject state to which Job is himself reduced (vv. 29, 30)—and yet Job never is abject! In an age when mental illness is widespread, this Book of Job is a mighty encouragement to many, for it gives them sure hope that they shall not snap under strain. Ere we reach verse 25 he will be rid of the "grues" and will again remember pity, even when he seems unpitied.

Once before Job had shown acquaintance with the unfortunate (24:4-11), but in that place he had shown them as victims of other men's greed and exploitation. Here they are vagabonds, delineated in words too painful.

The group or herd of outcasts, living on grasses and roots, "scourged out of the land," form a sort of gallery mocking Job, in verses 9-15. Here comes the deepest pain of contempt, and the only parallel to it is the crowning indignity described in Isaiah

50:6 and 53:3. Indeed it begins to appear that Job is a representative here of the supreme Sufferer, who from highest exaltation went to meet shame and spitting from Herod's court minions and Pilate's dicing soldiers and the fanatically enflamed Jews. What made the scum of society deal so arrogantly with Job was precisely their sense of superiority to one who in their eyes seemed smitten by God and afflicted. Verses 10, 11 appear to have this meaning. In the following verses there are mounts or siege-works "cast up" (12c), which remind us of the passage in 16:7-14, which forms the best commentary here. Dimly we discern behind the wild creatures of earth that other Antagonist who is the torture of Job's diseased imaginaion. That is why he describes "terrors" that are turned upon him, like hounds (cp. 6:4) or a besieging army breaking through, pitiless and irresistible (v. 14).

Echoes of Isaiah 53 occur in the last two sections of the chapter, as when "now is my soul poured out" recalls Isaiah 53:12. Whatever vagueness the description has, making translation so uncertain, is perhaps due to the uniqueness of the trial. The sufferer was emaciated and at the same time swollen and puffy so that his garment caught and constricted him (v. 18).

But the central agony, shown in verses 19-23, is the baffling silence of God. It is not even God's absence that hurts: worse is the sense of His hostile and angry presence. Tossed on the wind, *dissolved* in the storm, Job feels the contradiction of being and not being (v. 22). And now in a very different context of thought from Chapter 3 he contemplates dissolution which yet will be in the "meeting place" or house appointed for all living. Unfathomable woe—yet, as verse 24 will say, should not a man stretch out the hand, and appeal for help?

Disappointed, receiving evil where he had given good to others, appointed to darkness where he belonged to the light, this man of sorrows inevitably carries our thought to Some One else, One who was not so vocal—or when He did try to foretell His lonely sorrow, found no ear willing to hear.

JOB'S FINAL SPEECH, A SOLEMN CLAIM "NOT GUILTY," Chapter 31

31:1-4. God's all-seeing eye compelled me in youth to "make a covenant" with my own eyes. The disastrousness of evil desire, thought, and act confirmed my inner faith.

5-8. All that was showy but dishonest, I turned away from.

9-12. Adultery seemed to me a heinous crime, a destroying fire.
13-15. Harshness to the underprivileged showed up for what it is—an insult to God who made both that man and me.
16-23. Hardness of heart toward the defenseless poor, or selfish enjoyment that never took note of what others lacked—a sense of the majesty of God made these impossible for me.
24-40. To place my confidence in *things,* or in mysterious raptures of sense and mind—to take malicious pleasure in the downfall of men who disliked me, or to harbor miserly thoughts, or shyness when strangers needed hospitality—to follow face-saving devices, intimidated by the codes of successful people—all these things I repudiate, and land-grabbing, exploitation and eviction too.

Four times Job explicitly calls down upon himself dire consequences if he is speaking as a hypocrite (at vv. 8, 10, 22, 40), but at verses 28, 30, 32 and 35 Job's entire adherence to the exact opposite in conduct conveys the same point.

"As a prince," holding his head high, Job asks for the chance to come before God and claim a complete acquittal. That oft-repeated, "Oh, that," now sounds from Job's lips for the last time: "Oh, that I had one to hear me!" (vv. 35-40). If only the charge or accusation against Job were delivered into his hands, he would proudly take it and carry it on his shoulder, unabashed. Here faith again triumphs over anguished dismay, for it is faith, faith nourished from his past experience of God and surviving all appearances that might quench it, which comes to expression here. Job's attitude is not defiance, as was that of Prometheus, despite the "as a prince" approach to it. "Job, on his dung-heap, torn not by an eagle but by leprosy, defies the sufferings which almost overwhelm him to rob him of his faith in a hidden God" (H. W. Robinson). For a time Job had yielded to the temptation to count God unjust: now he is saying, "Great, just, good God," saying it by hope that has conquered despair.

Further study of the chapter, section by section, yields profit from two points of view: 1. by an examination of the ethical standards which Job counted unquestionably authoritative; and 2. because these settled minimum convictions of right and wrong became for Job, as he uttered them, a declaration and a defense of his faith in God. Stating the rules of living by which he had been steered through life, Job had been describing by implication the kind of God in whom he believed. He hardly realised what good he was doing to his own soul. He was a true *defensor fidei*, though still somewhat over-assertive, in verses 35-37, in defending himself.

The opening verses of the chapter show that pervasive sense of God and the "categorical imperative" of holding fast to His steps and keeping His way which had been stated at 23:10, 11. Is there, in fact, any basis for faith so strong as the moral basis? For all his seeming independence, this is where Job is in the grip of God. Faith is for him not an option but a necessity. Life is for Job meaningful only in terms of goodness. God is good. The two strands, ethical and theological, are interwoven through this crucial chapter.

God is of purer eyes than to behold iniquity, and deep interest attaches to Job's early abhorrence of flagrant sexual offense. It is a by-product of his awareness of the holiness of God. Verses 11, 12 show the seriousness of this disruptive and destructive surrender to desire. Verse 9 following upon verse 1 describes its growth; and in verse 10 Job as a just man faces the consequences of indulgence that could fairly come home to roost with him.

Next to Job's chastity is his inbred distaste, God-begotten too, for falsehood and deceit (cp. v. 6 with v. 2). These vices are spoken of as companions, pictured maybe as the knowing ones who are so eager to help simpletons to strike it rich! Job was never inflamed by their promises and "inside information," so he never chased after Deceit, in hot pursuit. Here, as in the fight for chastity, the heart is described as being stirred to cupidity by a message flashed from the eyes (v. 7). This man of integrity looks facts in the face and says, If I have deprived others of what was theirs, then let me see others eating what I had toiled to produce (v. 8).

To the sin of covetousness Job will return in verses 24, 25, but probably greed has been the root sin of the intervening verses from 13 to 23. Insufficient payment to workers or lack of sympathy with their just claims is mentioned first, and as before the situation is viewed as with God looking on. Once again, at verse 23 as in verse 14, God is seen as presiding over all the actions of a man with his fellows. Ungenerous behavior to the poor, neglect of Lazarus while I eat my morsel alone, and unfeeling disregard of the widow and the needy who require a fleece to warm them and something to eat—these evasions, says Job, I was powerless to practice! God saw to it (v. 23).

From beginning to end Job's high ethical standards take their rise and exercise authority *from God.* There is no humanism here, and no religionless morality. At the opposite end, Job is a witness that unethical Christians have not earned the moral right to affirm that they believe in God. Goodness is Job's anchorage in God: he had seen God—how else had he been pure in heart?

What has been called "cosmic emotion" is described in verses 26, 27, but it is not faith in God. A "wonderful feeling" in the senses or a soulful emotion may bring "uplift" yet remain quite pagan. Kissing the hand in worship of the heavenly bodies— a mystic sense of beauty, as some aesthetic persons would call it—would in Job's eyes have been a denial of the God that is above (v. 28).

Vindictive delight in the discomfiture of people who have shown malice to me, or even the inner wish for mischief to befall them—and as though nothing more need be said, Job leaves the sentence unfinished (vv. 29, 30). Maybe there is suspense and a climax is to come after inhospitable meanness and then social cowardice have also been mentioned, but in actual fact there is no further "then" to serve as an oath to establish his sincerity. Instead there is an expressed longing to come and appear before God (cp. Ps. 42:2), perhaps a little haughtily, and the closing words are about the soil Job had farmed, wondering if the mute earth was perhaps the plaintiff against him in these hidden charges against him of which he desires to be informed (cp. 16:18).

And with that last guess at what his mysterious guilt may be the words of Job are ended.

The Intervention of Elihu, Chapters 32-37

"Job's friends," wrote Strahan, "have a kind of fanatical belief in the greatness of God and the worthlessness of man," whereas Job's agony of mind lies in this, that "so long as he doubts whether God is infinitely good as well as great, he is in spiritual darkness."

The three friends have failed to help Job. They almost succeeded in doing what all the catastrophes which befell Job were unable to do. And now six chapters are added and a representative of the younger generation speaks. Is his contribution as final as he thought it would be? No. The last word is with God, and not as the solution of a problem, but in self-disclosure and fellowship that satisfy the soul. Job's cry for the appearance of God "had too many elements of challenge in it, as if the creature had the right to cite and interrogate his Maker." Who is to say, therefore, whether an interval between the human cry and the Divine answer was not appropriate? It was occupied by a faulty preacher, but even he (as the earlier Davidson pointed out) is a reminder to preachers that our work is only a clearing of the ground: "only God himself can convert by personal contact with the heart."

Elihu then is to be accepted, and the Book of Job interpreted as a whole. Fascinating as it may be to speculate about Elihu as representing a much later generation than could have spoken to Job, and to find reasons for regarding his speeches as a later insertion, an interruption, too, which postpones the dramatic climax of God's appearing, "we are entitled and under obligation in interpreting any book to consider the form in which it now appears.... Scripture having now in our days attained its full growth, it is with this full growth mainly that we have to do. ... In hermeneutics a first principle is to accept what we find in Scripture" (Comm. 1862, x, xi, xxxii).

Elihu's answers: (1) God is great but good. He is not arbitrary nor inscrutable in the sense you declare. God does speak (chaps. 32, 33). (2) God's justice, being basic to all that checks anarchy, is perfect. When afflicted, wait patiently, seek Him penitently, making response (chaps. 34, 35). (3) God's Providence is not so inscrutable. Suffering is educative: Who is a Teacher like Him? (36:1-23). (4) God's Unsearchable Greatness is demonstrated—Hark! Look!—in majesty and power (36:24—37:24). (The first signs of the approaching storm, the whirlwind.)

ELIHU'S APOLOGY AND INTRODUCTORY WORDS,
Chapter 32

32:1-5. Prose transition, introducing Elihu the indignant.
6-10. Young as I am, I ask for your attention, for youth, too, may be taught by the Almighty's inspiration.
11-14. Listening attentively to you older men, I was disappointed. You must not suppose Job invincible and leave him for God to deal with. What he will now hear is different.
15-22. (A soliloquy). Speechless, they admit defeat. Why then should I repress what surges within me? With regard for truth alone, and no flattery, I will speak.

We must beware of labelling Elihu as the "angry young man" of our Western world. There are differences of outlook and taste, and a different sense of humor between East and West, in Africa, too. To other peoples it does not seem bombastic if a speaker makes a long preamble to his speech. Elihu does this four times. The explosion of indignation (vv. 18, 19), is a necessary reminder of the young man's long restraint and serves to expose how completely unsuitable was the attempted answer by the friends.

Job was righteous in his own eyes: he justified himself rather than God—this, says the author, was what kindled the wrath of Elihu. The young man is therefore introduced with respect. He is a champion of more reverence in pondering God's ways. He would not seem ridiculous to the profound sense of "otherness" which Orientals have in their thought of God, especially when he seeks to "justify the ways of God to men." His deference to old age yields before his concern for God's honor, the more so because he is aware of wisdom given to him by the breath of the Almighty. "There was none that convinced Job"—therefore he felt thrust forward (v. 12).

His description of himself occurs in the soliloquy (note this!) as "bursting" with words and with the constraint to speak. "I am full of words" is intended to indicate how shocked he feels because the case for God has been abandoned by the older men. Even the ferment of wine in wine-skins is not comic: Elihu is driven on by the sense of how much more there is to say for God.

GOD IS NOT SILENT: HE GRACIOUSLY SPEAKS AND WORKS, Chapter 33

33:1-12. Job, you are wrong when you say, "I am innocent . . . and HE is looking for trouble with me." Your complaint is misdirected and misconceived. God is greater than man (v. 12).

13-33. God is not silent nor indifferent. In two ways He speaks: By dream or vision, and by painful illness. His aim is to wean men from self-will and self-destruction. A heavenly messenger persuasively woos and awakens the soul—repentance is God's means of rescue, and life begins anew. The redeemed soul gives joyous testimony.

Far from being silent, "God speaketh once, yea twice." Far from being inactive in grace, "all these things doth God work, twice, yea thrice." This is the message of Elihu, and he unfolds the purpose of God as being to draw man back from proud independence, in order that his life may be renewed—"his flesh shall be fresher than a child's." God's marvellous and merciful kindness is the theme.

Elihu answers Job's request for an intermediary, some one less overwhelming than God, less awe-inspiring—"I also am formed out of the clay" (v. 6). When later Elihu mentions "an interpreter" of heavenly power and authority who stirs effectual longing within a human soul, so that it truly repents, it is difficult not to think of these two aspects of the full Christian gospel —an Incarnation plus the inward operations of the Holy Spirit— as being foreshadowed here. The surprise would rather be if there were *not* echoes and intuitions within earnest souls in earlier generations. And in a context where the deepest need of men and God's readiness to pardon and renew the soul are being treated, how appropriate that a man claiming awareness of the Spirit of God should speak with overtones! This remains true even if the words, "I have found a ransom," must in its context be construed as meaning primarily, "a means of rescue" (cp. 36:18).

It will be noted that Elihu claims no superiority, but stands "toward God" on a level with Job, not exerting "pressure" such as would tilt the scales against him. Yet the dignity of manhood, perhaps also the mysterious prerogative of being quickened by the "breath of God," inspires him with confidence in speaking to another man, another being who is animated and can be effectually awakened by the Divine Spirit. For the time being Elihu passes over at verse 12 the greatness of God. His first concern is to show God active in grace, God speaking. It is Job's complaint of God's silence that is taken up at verse 13.

Dreams and visions are the first means of communication used by God that he mentions. This was the thought which left Eliphaz breathless (4:12-19). Eliphaz widened the gulf between God and men, but Elihu seeks to close it. God is shown as the seeker. His concern is to keep back man's soul from the pit of destruction. The saving God is not remote and indifferent. Thrice the urgency of salvation and the danger of man is mentioned —in verses 18, 28, 30. "He openeth the ears of men," for God is persistent and unwearied. "He tries one way after another," is Strahan's rendering of "once, yea twice" and "twice, yea thrice." God is determined to withdraw man from all purposes of his that run counter to God's purpose.

The remedial activity of God, as well as His redemptive action, is elaborated in the description of pain upon his bed (v. 19). "He is chastened," says Elihu, thus stating the disciplinary and reformative ministry of suffering. Yet pain in itself is not guaranteed to bring blessing. Along with it there has to be some one to "show unto man what is right for him" (v. 13). Few passages even of Scripture have such beauty as those describing the acceptance and realisation of personal salvation in verses 25-28, but compare 5:17-27. "He prayeth unto God" reminds us of Acts 9:11. "He seeth His face with joy" involved in old time coming into God's house with sacrifice, and sacrifice is consummated in praise (v. 26). "He singeth before men"—this gives the communal expression which a liberated soul desires, and it does not now hesitate to make confession: "I have sinned and perverted that which was right, and it profited me not" (v. 27).

Here Elihu, alas, is not on such solid ground as Hosea 14:2 in urging Job to accept the form of words for confession. Elihu still takes the view that Job in justifying himself needs to be searched out (see 34:36). Therefore Elihu's words in verse 32, "I desire to justify thee," cannot mean that he stands with Job (see 34:7-9). What was written of a Greater One still holds true of Job: "Of the people there was none with him." More than anyone knew, the Intermediary still must be God alone, and how He shall be also man, standing at Job's side, is yet to be disclosed. Elihu cherished dreams, as we shall see again, that were not to be fulfilled by him. The last word will be with *God*.

ELIHU JUSTIFIES GOD AND CONDEMNS JOB, Chapter 34

34:1-15. "Yea, of a surety *God* will not do wickedly, neither will the *Almighty* pervert justice." (Addressed to wise men.)

16-20. "Without justice rule is impossible, and therefore injustice in the supreme Ruler is inconceivable" (Davidson). (Addressed, like that which follows, to Job.)

21-28. Nothing is hidden from God: does He then need to investigate any case? Mighty men are supplanted and overturned; why? They had turned aside from God and oppressed the poor.

29-33 God is to be trusted when He bestows peace or withholds His favor, either to nation or individual: He has their interest at heart. It is presumptuous for anyone to insist that God should answer him either to show what his sin was or to conform the treatment of him to what the man chooses.

34-37. The verdict of the wise is to condemn Job's speeches. To the sin of his former life he has now added the rebellious, unsubmissive attitude, in a defiant gesture of scorning God among us.

At 33:9-11 and again at 34:5, 6 Job's words are quoted (from 9:21; 10:7; 16:17; 23:10 and 27:5). In that delineation of God, Job has occupied the place of the scornful. Elihu classes him with the hardened wicked of Psalm 1:1. He has affirmed that God is unrighteous and declared his own righteousness (13:18). A third charge mentioned at verse 9 was actually the opposite of what Job's attitude had been; he had lifted up his face without spot to God when life had stripped him bare. But Elihu fastens on his descriptions of the prosperity of the wicked—exaggerated as these were—and wrongly attributed to Job a hankering after the way of the wicked.

Elihu therefore starts off with a sweeping verdict: a judge giving his verdict before examining the evidence! The "wise men" he is addressing are reckoned to be onlookers.

Again at verse 10 Elihu speaks to that jury of men of understanding whose estimate he will pre-judge in verses 34, 35. In verse 11 Elihu follows Bildad in contradicting the assertion that God makes men suffer beyond their deserts (G. B. Gray). Utterly uncompromising is Elihu's thesis in verse 12, "uttered twice with strong emphasis and great solemnity": "Yea, of a surety *God* will not do wickedly, neither will the *Almighty* pervert justice." Not being anyone's deputy, He rules the earth and is "answerable to none" (cp. 36:23b; Gray). Paul says the same in Romans 9:14. Kelly puts the point well by reminding us "that the idea of God and the idea of wickedness are not compatible." The total dependence of man upon God shown in God's creatorship carries also the assurance of His benevolence, for if God were to gather man's breath or spirit back to Himself, all flesh would perish together and man would return unto dust (vv. 14, 15).

What will follow from Elihu's lips will be faulty from the standpoint of formal logic, but though he will "beg the question" in verse 17 ff. the presuppositions of his thinking and belief as now stated are impregnable, and will be confirmed in Job's experience after encountering God, just as they were shown to be inwoven with his inmost being in his closing "oath of clearance."

Whereas Job followed what we call the inductive method,

looking at the facts of life and drawing his own conclusions, Elihu, like the friends, starts with the presuppositions inherent in Godhead. Verse 16 shows that he does not expect contradiction to his argument. In its own way, it is a fair contention, based on deep conviction of the inherent character, not this time of the Creator, but of the moral Ruler of the universe. The fact that God does, in fact, govern the world declares His hatred of misgovernment as He sees it in men (or angels) (vv. 19, 20). The verdict God passes on a king or on nobles, checking perversity or wickedness in them, confirms the thought that injustice is not to be thought of in the supreme Ruler (v. 18). It is verse 17b which "begs the question" and ominously echoes 12:16-25 as speaking unrighteously for God (13:7, 8). That long passage quoted back to the friends by Job had led Job to dismiss them as incompetent to judge his case because intimidated by sheer power, they were men willing to distort the truth in fear of the Divine majesty. For the question in debate is whether God the mighty One is also the just One, and therefore the answer, "God is the mighty just One" (unless it is developed), only takes us back to the beginning, before the question was asked. In 36:3b Elihu will again "ascribe righteousness to his Maker," but it is wholesome to remember two things: (1). At the end God will completely ignore Elihu's contribution; and (2). The arguments of the friends (and here Elihu is only repeating these) are declared not to be right in the way Job's statements are right.

Elihu is on surer ground when in verses 21-30 he describes God as active within His world, developing the suggestive phrase in verse 20, "the mighty are taken away *without hand*" (by unseen power that is not human, cp. Dan. 2:34, 35; Zech. 4:6). The decline and fall of empires illustrate the point well, at least in the retrospect, yet sometimes also dramatically, as in A.D. 1945. "He overturneth them in the night" almost becomes "in a night" sometimes, and it is shown (though Pharaoh's disastrous night is not mentioned) that the cry of the afflicted does reach God's ear.

The other point Elihu makes at verse 23 refers back to Job's claim to come before God (23:3, 4), to be heard and given the reason for God's strange treatment of him. Job, however, as Gray reminds us, "has anticipated Elihu in pointing out that as a matter of fact God and man do not meet at a tribunal, 9:32f." Elihu declares that God is never under-informed about anyone, needs no commission of inquiry. "Past finding out" is misleading as a translation of verse 24, for the context demands "without investigation." Without the need for further investigation, God shatters the mighty, is the meaning.

This has been a difficult chapter, and the sequence of thought in verses 29-33 is notably teasing. Follow the analysis given above, for verses 29, 30. Verse 31 commends the attitude of penitence, and is followed by a plea for humility and teachableness. A rebuke to Job for presuming to dictate to God is sharply administered in verse 33, and Elihu finishes on a harsh note. The end takes us back to verses 7-9, and there a quite ludicrous picture of Job, as a sort of Falstaffian Voltaire taking deep draughts of sarcasms against God, is depicted. Elihu talks of Job as eager to find companions in wickedness (v. 8), and is not scrupulous about accuracy or fairness in verse 9. He was actually saying the jibe from Satan about Job which God denied. Strange that men with sublime eloquence about God should be so unjust when they declare God's justice. There is probably an extravagant rhetorical flourish in Elihu's pretension that Job is openly mocking at God by clapping his hands.

THE PRECEPTOR EXAMINES HIS PUPIL, Chapter 35

35:1-8. Have you really any right to complain against God? "Behold the skies . . . higher than thou!" It is not God but men who benefit by your goodness or are hurt by your wickedness.

9-16. Under oppression men cry out to God (God as supreme Arbiter is always there, in Elihu's thought). Claiming to be innocent, you, too, cry out, and say you are not answered. There is a reason: pride and dislike of God's instruction make your cry void. You are not looking truly to God who gives songs in the night; but He gives them to those who respond.

Elihu has the mind of an educator, and does painstakingly take up Job point by point. Note "Thou sayest" in verse 3 and in verse 14, for these are pivotal to the two sections of this chapter. While the transcendence of God leaves him awed and sometimes overinclined to stress the independence of God (beyond criticism), and he quotes from or repeats Eliphaz a great deal, yet he is fascinated by the ways of God as man's Teacher (33:13-33; 36:22; 37:19). "That which I see not, teach thou me" had been his prescribed prayer to Job in 34:32.

At 34:9 Elihu had referred in passing to a point which he now takes up again and develops—whether profit was derived by Job from godliness. How best to express from verse 3 what "this" means in verse 2 is not easy; possibly Elihu had his own ideas and was not over-precise in verse 2b when quoting Job. But, "thou sayest," clarifies the reader's grasp of Elihu's answer: What "advantage" or "profit" has Job derived? Eliphaz in 22:2-4 had not very convincingly touched on this, and 22:12 starts Elihu off on the same trail at 35:5. A fleeting thought of Job's at 7:20 raised the question, "If I have sinned, what do I unto thee, O thou Watcher of men?" To suspect Job of wavering in his moral loyalties, however, was the mistake of all four "partisans" of God in this book, just as their suspicions of Jesus and His motives proved to be the incredible blindness of the Pharisees. "Far be it from God that he should do wickedness" had been a sound argument in 34:10 though not so well used by Elihu as by Abraham (Gen. 18:25). Elihu hardly dreamed of the profit that might have come to Job by his intercession. When he does turn to the subject of prayer, it is in a doctrinaire spirit arguing a point, but not touched with a feeling of others' infirmities, still less his own.

If the argument of verses 9-16 is earthenware, however, there is a treasure within the drab setting. A glimpse of the Divine grace and glory comes, as often, in the thought or diction of this defender of God's honor. "Thou sayest thou beholdest him not" is Elihu's reference back to 23:3, 8, 9—that classic yearning for God given imperishable expression in, "Oh, that I knew where I might find him!" But Elihu, without grasping the longing for God which Job felt, and even in schoolmasterly fashion disqualifying Job from expectation of an answer from God to praying by such as him, drops this pearl, this question that is better than information and more inspiring than argument: "Where is God my maker, who giveth songs in the night?"

The lofty One of these four wise men is certainly the God we adore. The God who gives beauty for ashes and the garment of praise for the spirit of heaviness and songs in the night is no less the God we adore. Why should men who speak for God prove to be so often one-eyed and one-handed?

Elihu's third speech ends with the spurning attitude now familiar. Here are his points: Who teacheth us more than beasts can be taught? But instruction is restricted, we have just implied, to those who are teachable. Job, by insisting on calling God to order, and declaring, forsooth, that he is waiting for God to answer him, demonstrates his incorrigible arrogance. Little does he appreciate the self-restraint God exercises in his case, and so he talks on and on!

GOD'S TEACHING IS BY CORRECTION, Chapter 36:1-23

36:1-4. Elihu's introduction, stating his qualifications.
    5-16. God is mighty and to Him no soul or life can be a paltry thing. His treatment of men is never indiscriminate. The response determines the result for good or ill.
   17-23. Impatience against so incomparable a Teacher, refusal to realise how indispensable suffering is—this can only mean that your heart is set on iniquity. Otherwise you would have consented to affliction, and benefitted from His correction.

The two remaining subjects with which Elihu proposes to deal are indicated in verse 5. The first will occupy most of the present chapter: "God is mighty, and despiseth not any." The second is treated from verse 24 and through all of Chapter 37: "God is mighty in strength of understanding." In its turn this closing treatment of the Divine wisdom forms an introduction to God's intervention out of the whirlwind (chaps. 38-41).

The comprehensive erudition which Elihu in his manner claims is certainly the impressive characteristic not of Elihu but of the author of this book. That will appear most of all in the last chapters, but meantime the author is perhaps to be conceived as having found his own motto in Elihu's words at verse 24, "Remember that thou magnify his work, whereof men have sung."

Punishment and correction in mercy through accepted affliction—this is the positive side of Elihu's message. Submissive souls are the "righteous" of verse 7. From them God does not withdraw His eyes, but He exalts them like kings. Everything depends, whether for kings or others "bound in fetters . . . taken in the cords of affliction" (although the description seems designed for kings), upon the readiness to acknowledge the heart's obstinacy. If the heart is teachable, God opens the heart to instruction. As all through Israel's history, so here the alternative is stated: "If they hearken. . . . If they hearken not" (vv. 11, 12).

The stubborn resist God, and the fate of these godless is given in verses 13, 14 just as the other friends had unequivocally stated it—"they die in youth."

The return journey from the far country is a subject on which the speaker's heart is warm. "Return" is the Old Testament word for repentance or being converted, and both the preparatory disposition ("He openeth their ear") and the sway exercised over the will ("He commandeth that they return from iniquity") are brought out in verse 10. As though Job's time for a true change of mind seems past, yet not in despair, Elihu speaks home to Job from verse 16, "Yea, he would have allured thee out of distress into a broad place." Viands on the table are "full of fatness" (v. 16). Pleasantness, the marginal reading in verse 11c, is one of the notes struck musically by the "wise men" (cp. Prov. 3:17), so it is combined as an allurement in a section which holds more of warning (vv. 17-23).

Verse 18 sums up the entreaty and the solemn warning together. It is important to grasp its full meaning. Wrathful impatience was by the friends reckoned Job's besetting sin, so he is urged not to allow wrath to drive him into irreverence or mockery (E.R.V. marg.) "neither let the greatness of the ransom turn thee aside." The word used in 33:24 is more clear still here from the context: the "ransom" is the costly acceptance of severe suffering as God's pathway of restoration. Job must not allow himself to be deflected, otherwise he would be choosing the night (v. 20), which is reckoned to be the disastrous time in which an entire people are cut off. In the New Testament the midnight cry likewise is a catastrophic disclosure of unreadiness for many.

Among many gleaming sayings of simple brevity unexpectedly occurring in Elihu's speeches, and as persuasive as anything he ever said to Job, comes this: "Behold, God doeth loftily in his power; who is a teacher like unto him?"

And this makes also the transition to the final section of his speech about the power and greatness of God. It is prepared for in verse 24 and launched at verse 26.

ELIHU EXTOLS THE WONDROUS WORKS OF GOD
Chapters 36:24—37:24

36:24-33. "Behold, God is great. . . . Behold, he spreadeth his light around him."
37:1-13. "Hear, oh, hear the noise of his voice. . . . God thundereth marvellously."
37:14-24. "Hearken unto this, O Job. Stand still and consider."

Although it will not equal in power the Divine descriptive

vividness and finished brevity in the following speech, Elihu's peroration reaches sublimity. There are sentences that arrest like a vista which makes a climber stop, and there are phrases which bring to view remembered peaks which received all their majesty from a court-scene of clouds. The passing wind which clears the sky of clouds—just like that!—and the beasts going into their coverts to hibernate, and "golden splendor" coming out of the north, and the lightning like an arrow speeding to strike its target—all these are immediate pictures before the mind's eye.

The whole section vibrates with an excitement that throbs through the diction. "Behold . . . behold . . ." (that word occurred four times in chap. 36) and "Listen, oh, listen" (as Moffatt puts it in 37:2) is intensified still further in 37:14 with "Hearken . . . stand still . . . consider the wondrous works of God." Imagination kindles, and the eye stimulates the ear, then the heart bows in awe, for "God hath upon him terrible majesty."

Not a finished artist (note how 36:29 is not left perfectly touched, but the artist has to try again at 37:16), Elihu is too surprised and exalted to do much more than exclaim. Rather than attempt to analyse, we ought to catch his mood, and aim to see what he sees and listen as he does. The sky, the atmosphere, rains that are so "mighty" that man's field work is closed down, clouds which pour down, yes, and note distillation in verse 27 —these and the ice formed by the breath of God (an unparalleled reference to that breath) but mainly the thunder of God's voice, are set before us with a poet's eye.

The moralist re-enters at verse 13 with mention of "correction," and presses home his point at verses 15, 16 asking "dost thou know?" Lightning had been in the sky, thunder had rolled and crashed, then deep darkness had enveloped the scene (v. 19). As Moulton helpfully indicates by marginal notes in *The Modern Reader's Bible*, there had been a loud peal of thunder at 37:1, causing Elihu to say, "At this also my heart trembles, and leaps out of its place."

Before 37:14 Moulton further adds, "The storm has become a whirlwind, with thick darkness and flashes of lightning." It is in this awesome environment of cloud, and majesty, and awe that Elihu puts to Job a question: "Should a man wish that he were swallowed up?"

Yet, clothed as He is with terrible majesty, God at his appearing is going to astound all those who hear, to astound yet not overpower them. And no one afterwards will say "I told you so!"

The Answer of the Almighty, Chapters 38—41

It is out of the whirlwind that God speaks. This, of course, means that His answer is solemnising. It is *God* who speaks, as Elijah, Ezekiel and Zechariah discovered, and the writer of Psalm 29 (I Kings 19:11ff.; Ezek. 1:4ff.; Zech. 9:14).

Some readers will be disappointed at first. They may find the whole speech "astonishing alike in its irony and in its seeming irrelevance. . . . It seems at first a totally unethical answer to an intensely ethical problem."

No charge of Divine intimidation may be brought, however, for in the Bible God's ways are so fascinating just because they are so full of surprises. After Ezekiel's terrifying, overwhelming vision of the storm-cloud and the Divine glory at the heart of it, the prophet lay prostrate on his face. The voice that spoke said, "Son of man, stand upon thy feet, and I will speak unto thee." Exactly so God here speaks to Job: "Gird up now thy loins like a man." There is nearness and respect for manhood, as well as Divine omnipotence, and this is interesting.

The next surprise, however, is that God turns attention away from humankind altogether. It is to the height, and breadth, and depth of the universe in space that He first summons Job, so that immediately after the words, "Gird up thy loins like a man," he is taken through some regions "where no man is" (38:26). Earth, ocean, the coming of the dawn, snow, rain, ice and frost are mentioned, and then the orderliness of the orbits of the planets, and the mystery of clouds which pour down plentiful rain, with lightnings to announce its coming. After this survey of inanimate creation, Job is brought to consider the wonders of the animal world, but "here, as there, it is not the exceptional things, but everything, that is wonderful—the ox, the ass, the goat, the horse, the hawk, the lion, and behind them all the wonderful love of God."

But that wonderful love is implicit as yet, becoming explicit, but demanding an attentive mind. How then does the answer come? The mind has its part to play (to us who read the same injunction comes)—"Gird up now thy loins like a man" (for neither physics nor biology fail to yield impressive facts and great imponderables also). Yet the secret God will unveil "is a bright and not a sad one," for as G. K. Chesterton further said, when we are told about the laying of the foundations of the world, "all the sons of God shouted for joy," "one cannot help feeling that they had something to shout about." Meantime Job is like young Isaiah: in discovering that the fulness of the whole earth is God's manifestation in glory, there is more than intellectual illumination. God's full answer is more than the solution of an immediate problem, for God acts "by flushing all the channels of thought and life with a deeper sense of Himself. Under the flow of this fuller sense of God perplexities disappear, just as rocks that raise an angry surf when the tide is low are covered and unknown when it is full."

Job's reply will be, "Now mine eye seeth Thee," and the assurance is full of wonder and rest, not in spite of the penitence that marks its entrance but precisely because of the deeper sense of sin. God's healing is always more than a cure, and when God came He came to rebuke and to heal. The quality God most looks for is teachableness, and in Job's case teachableness involved the discovery that the presuppositions he had nourished involved him in a long and painful process of unlearning before he could learn aright.

The last two chapters of the answer of the Almighty are less full of grandeur and sublimity than the first two, and yet they are appropriate in what we might call a more relaxed sense. The two formidable creatures with which Job is confronted, as though he were primeval man, only underline a lesson pervasively present from the start of God's questions, namely man's limited cognition, but just as much man's limited control. The wild ass is untrammeled and free; the wild ox cannot be bound and made to drive a furrow; and even the feckless ostrich outstrips the horse and his rider.

Yet the aim of all this is not abasement and humiliation but humility, perhaps one might add, good humored humility, and the restoring of mind as well as soul. Job's discovery is this, that "God is his redeemer not merely out of existing sorrows or in spite of them, but in them and through them and by means of them."

JOB IS ANSWERED OUT OF THE STORM, Chapter 38:1–38

38:1-3. The voice of majesty, rebuke and mercy.
4-38. Survey of the earth in space; subjects—the earth, the sea, coming of the dawn, the deepest depths (vv. 4-18); the celestial treasuries from which come light, snow, lightning, and rain (vv. 19-30); stars, constellations and clouds (vv. 31-38).

It has often been noted that the speech of the Lord (note the covenant name Jehovah) claims close attention for what God leaves unsaid almost as much as for what He says. A full answer to the mystery of suffering—*could* that be given, since we are to walk by faith, not by sight? Calvary will be the biggest possible answer, but there, too, it is in the terms of faith. Intelligence, however, is not thrust out of court, nor treated in any cavalier fashion. On the contrary, it is honored and exalted here. God asks for a greater employment of it.

"*Consider,*" said the Lord Jesus Christ, pointing to flowers of the field and birds of the air. "*Perceive* ye not yet, neither *understand?*" This was constantly the appeal of the Son of God, and His illustrations were drawn from the Father's workings in the world around us. Thus we must conclude that sometimes God must speak out of a whirlwind in order to draw our attention to the regular processes of seedtime and harvest, summer and winter, day and night. The surprising things God does in majesty and awe direct our eyes and thoughts to His normal mercies which really are breath-taking.

What was necessary, God knew how to supply. Says Chesterton, "Job was comfortless before the speech of Jehovah and is comforted after it. He has been told nothing, but he feels the terrible and tingling atmosphere of something which is too good to be told." It is a startling universe in which we live, and meantime God is content to direct Job's eyes outward. What a mind-cure that can be! Chesterton, who had that great capacity for laughter which turns defense of the faith into attack, says of this section of the Book of Job that in it God "seems to say that if it comes to asking questions, He can ask some questions that will fling down and flatten out all conceivable human questioners." Is this a frontal attack on our unbelief, or does God turn our flank?

The wonderful thing is that the roar of the storm subsides (we are not told that it does), and Job hears himself being called by name. Immediately after the comfort of that personal call there follows a disturbing question: "Who is this. . . ?" and the charge is twofold. First, ignorance, and next that he is obscuring the counsel or design of God. Job was a man with a passion for facts and evidence, but how little he has seen! How he has distorted the picture and hid from view its meaning! Nevertheless God does not ask him to grovel, but as with Ezekiel, to stand to it "like a man."

The proper study of mankind—as Pope might here have learned

—is the ways of God, His works in creation and providence, and thus in grace also.

First God takes the foundation-laying of the earth, and startles Job by asking, "Were you there?" or, rather, "Where wast thou?" That foundation-laying was a notable occasion. Every measurement showed precision, and the pillars fitted in the sockets until the structure arose in perfection and the corner-stone was added. The architecture of the earth? Some readers may fail in visual images, but none can fail in auditory appreciation of the next words, "When the morning stars sang together, and all the sons of God shouted for joy."

In a striking second picture God refers to the birth of the ocean. Our puny minds are invited to think of the ocean as some enormous baby issuing from the womb. (Was it the womb of chaos from which it came, as popular folk-tales of the time said?) The strange baby was wrapped in a swaddling-band of thick darkness—the hidden horizon (seamen know what that means), and the garment added to it was made of clouds. Always unruly, the sea was made subject to God's decree and boundary (Prov. 8:29). Rock, or shingle, or the soft sand, silently or noisily declares God's ruling. "Hitherto shalt thou come, but no further: and here shall thy proud waves be stayed."

Third of the seven themes is the overspreading of earth by the dawn. The thought is of a coverlet of darkness being lifted off from the hills and valleys, lifted off at the corners as a cloth, while the wicked are shaken out, discomfited as all things stand forth in the light. And Job is asked whether it was at orders given by him that all this began to happen and has continued ever since!

Bathoscopes and other equipment for deep sea exploration are of recent invention, but God's next question is about the recesses or springs of the sea, and from there the thought travels to deeper depths, right to the gates of death. The previous paragraph started with, "Hast thou commanded the morning?" and here the question is, "Hast thou entered into the springs of the sea?" The great deep below the earth acts as couch or support (Gen. 49:25; Ps. 24:2; 136:6) but has Job reached it, or seen the gates of death? The question about the breadth of the earth and the depths beyond the deep sea gathers up all that has been surveyed on earth into the command: "Declare, if thou knowest it all." Every word has its sting.

And now it will be the celestial regions on which Job must submit to examination (vv. 19-38). Presumably Job was not the author of Chapter 28, but we can recognise divine inspiration behind both it and also Proverbs 8. Babylonians and Egyptians early had their own advanced wisdom, and of quite marvellous precision, for astronomy was an early interest of the wise, just as meteorological reports and rainfall were important for farmers. The present section with its three paragraphs, therefore, connects man's powers of observation and skill in deduction with the heavenly bodies and the treasuries or storehouses that hang in the sky—the clouds. (Wisdom is in vv. 36, 37.)

Light and darkness having been separated at the creation, they are reckoned as having distinct dwelling-places, and Job is asked if he has followed the pathway to each. The irony is strong in verse 21 when Job is treated as a contemporary with light, which Milton calls "offspring of heaven first born." It is from heaven also that snow comes, and hail. The covenant God of Israel refers to the day of battle and war in association with hail (Josh. 10:11) but snow at turning-points of later history has a connection also. These "treasuries" of frustration for powerful armies, of Napoleon and Hitler, for example, are given a forward view still in verse 23. They are "reserved against the time of trouble, the day of battle and war"—as though God already has in mind a final Armageddon, says Chesterton.

The questions proceed at verse 25, and how varied is the form of each! The downpour in a thunderstorm is at the other extreme from the drops of dew, and both differ from ice and hoary frost.

Yet pervading all the questions is the concern about origins. Were you there when earth's foundations were laid? Are you indeed a twin with light at the creation? And now comes the query, "Who hollowed a channel for the torrential downpour?" And again, "The hoary frost of heaven, who hath gendered it?" "Out of whose womb came the ice?" Additional to the interest in beginnings is the special feature of this portion in verses 26, 27—God's concern for places where the foot of man has never trod. It is He who sends "rain . . . on the wilderness, wherein there is no man." It is a rebuke to human arrogance. "A land where no man is" will receive comment later, for the second main half of God's message will be about the creatures man has not subdued, and the wilderness and salt land in which they live. Seals, walruses and polar bears might well have been under the ice in verse 30, but the main thought is that God sees to the wild creatures and the flowers in no-man's land, for He sends them rain though they have no address or visiting card.

The positions in the heavens of the stars at different times of the year bring the enquiry about the "ordinances of the heavens." But first the musical English names Pleiades and Orion recall us to the staggering question "Canst thou bind . . . or loose" their bands? Those two verbs are heavy with meaning for the church of Christ, and here the greatness of the prerogative involved is shown. "Some one does all these wonderful things; is it by any chance Job?"

"Canst thou" at verse 31 is repeated at verse 34: "Canst thou lift up thy voice to the clouds . . . send forth lightnings . . . pour out the bottles of heaven?" God has concern even for the dust of the earth, which runs into a mass when the rain makes the soil cohere. Agriculturists would agree that nothing in God's sight is insignificant.

In the context of this paragraph verse 36 has puzzled scholars. "Dark and deep cloud masses" are as likely as man's "inward parts" to be the place where God's wisdom is operative. Moreover 37:12 is a good clue to follow about clouds as showing wisdom inasmuch as "they do whatsoever He commandeth them." What is given "understanding" in verse 36b is hard to determine (the book of Job has an unusual number of uncertainties in the Hebrew text) but it may best be seen as something (mind or meteor or comet) that makes weather forecasts possible.

GOD'S CARE FOR WILD CREATURES, Chapters 38:39–39:30

The six sections describe lions and ravens, wild goats, the wild ass and wild ox, the ostrich, the horse, and the hawk and eagle. Features special to each of these groups adorn each paragraph and invite the reader to read and then examine all that is said.

The animate creation supplies a selection from God's casebook. First comes the hunger problem, and it is the young ones of the lion and the raven for which God is concerned to make provision. Their throats when hungry utter an unmistakable sound, the mouth yawning wide for food, and their cry is called a prayer to God. Lack of food—how dominating is the instinct in the lion and lioness, and how vivid is the picture of their quivering young, lying low yet intent on one thing only! Twice the word "prey" is used, as if to remind us that hunger is hunger, the great primal urge. Said the Lord Jesus, "Your heavenly Father feedeth them. Are not ye of much more value than they?"

Next to the widest, most constant instinct, hunger, God sees birth and procreation as the second call on Him for help. Doubtless the duration of "the months" that the animals fulfil—elephants so much longer than all others—is part of the question, but it focuses on the wild goat, because speedy delivery is so marked in them. Furthest from medical care, as we would now say, "they bow themselves, they cast out their pains." And shall not God, aware of the anguish of fear in human mothers, highly civilised or primitive, show a Creator's concern for that which has been curiously wrought, as Psalm 139 tells us, far away from human sight? But the question to Job is whether he even has the knowledge of animal differences sufficient to make him the curator of a small zoological garden.

A birth has taken place, but what then? Verse 4b supplies the interesting transition. The young ones grow up, "they go forth and return not again." That is exactly the characteristic of the wild ass, which is as free as the wind, almost. "The range of the mountains is his pasture," and the din of a city is something he scornfully rejects. The passion for freedom (one of Paul's great themes, and His Master's before him, Gal. 5:1, 13; John 8:32, 36) comes surprisingly to utterance in this context, but ought it to surprise us? God loves to liberate from every tyranny: the wild ass is to be congratulated because he "heareth not the shoutings of the driver" (marg. task-master). Similarly the wild ox roams at liberty (vv. 9-12). Untamed, he will neither harrow the valleys after you nor bring home your seed. These two creatures are very different from the domesticated ass and ox, and in their shy, uninhibited enjoyment of the wide spaces and every green thing their Creator takes delight.

Some commentators reckon the ostrich an intrusion here (it is absent from the Greek O.T.), in part because of the absence of questions and the giving of more than the usual amount of comment and information. (Is this really so?) On the other hand, the contradictions in her nature bring out something that we cannot do without. Swift as she is, with pinions waving proudly, she is feckless about her young and abandons her eggs on the earth. So at least the belief of the day ran, probably because an ostrich did not brood until the full complement of eggs was hatched (30 in number) or perhaps because during the incubation period she was seen to go in search of food. Anyhow, the ostrich had the habit of running in circles, and against the wind, not with it. The Arabian proverb was, "more foolish than an ostrich." Feckless but fleet of wing and foot—no question is asked about her. What stands out is this, in her disfavor: "she leaveth . . . and forgetteth . . . and dealeth hardly with her young ones." This unnatural behavior makes her stand out as almost too human! In Isaiah 49:15 a question is asked, and an answer is given: "Can a woman forget her sucking child? Yes, they may forget. . . . Yet will not I forget thee." The contrast between God and this outlandish bird described by current notions was certainly not missed by the listening Job. That God should permit such a creature to exist shows how little we understand His full design (vv. 13-18).

Now comes the only domesticated animal, man's greatest friend, the horse. "Hast thou given the horse" his qualities of strength, beauty, speed—and his astonishing flair for battle? No one who has seen an Arab horse galloping like the wind, and the white flowing robes of her rider streaming in the breeze, or has seen another well-trained animal jumping ("Leap as a locust," v. 20) can withhold admiration. What God said to Job about a horse may well catch the ear and the mind of thousands of men and women who love a horse.

Down the long centuries from ancient times when Israel's king was warned not to multiply horses, and to the vast stables that Solomon built, our mind travels irresistibly to medieval warfare and the vast weight of armor loaded on the patient horse—and the question that stays unanswered is this: Who was the wiser, the horse or his rider? "He mocketh at fear and is not dismayed." Need I be? Or shall I shrink when Christ summons me to war?

The final paragraph is about the soaring hawk and eagle, and the query runs, "Is it by thy wisdom. . . . Is it at thy command?" that they soar and mount. The hawk migrates southward at the approach of winter—did Job implant that mysterious instinct? The eagle (perhaps the word here and at 9:26 indicates a vulture, and the description better suits that bird) looks for an inaccessible crag of rock for nesting. "From thence she spieth out the prey. Her young ones also suck up blood." Job presumably gave hawk and vulture their being and characteristics—or would he perhaps not have called into existence creatures that prey on other creatures and suck up blood?

This forms the transition to Jehovah's challenge in Chapter 40, "Wilt thou condemn me?" If you can do things better, have a try!

GOD'S CHALLENGE: WHY NOT MOUNT THE THRONE?
Chapter 40

40:1-14. Discussion between the Lord and Job. Questions, and then, verses 9-14, a staggering invitation.

15-24. Behemoth, a creature of vast brute strength, imperturbable yet vigilant, is a "masterpiece" of God.

Job had said many things as if he were qualified to judge. The question now comes, "Wilt thou annul my judgment?" You see a quick way to abase the proud and tread down the wicked? You would do things so much better? Then why not try?

Thrice the word "answered" is used, twice of Jehovah, once of Job. "Shall a faultfinder maintain his contention with God?" is the first answer, and as usual God's answers take the form of questions. Next He will ask, "Wilt thou condemn me that thou mayest be justified?" The whole long discussion is therefore now under review. At once Job replies disclaiming any right or desire to open his mouth. "Once have I spoken . . . yea, twice." And what does it all add up to? How could he have lifted himself up to present a challenge to God?

As though that sort of reflection was induced in Job's mind by God, God first braces him as before with a reminder of his human dignity, and then raises again the Divine righteousness as the great issue which Job has called in question. The enforcement of justice in a world where so much wrong is done demands power, so verse 9 introduces the inquiry whether Job possesses power and majesty enough to crush the proud and make the wicked tremble.

Again the weapon used is irony—an ironical invitation to take over the sceptre of government, arrayed in the robes and regalia of majesty. Job has therefore to bring together two worlds—that great panorama of the creation outside of humankind which he has seen spread before him ("answer it" in v. 2 referred to that), and that other world of groans, oppressions, unrequited wrongs and excessive encouragements to wickedness, on which Job had spoken so knowingly. Job's answer is, "I lay my hand upon my mouth." The immediate and irrevocable overthrow of the evildoer as by a torrent of his anger is not in his power to achieve. The moral order of the world involves shutting within the dark prison-house of death (v. 13) the successful sinners

Job denounced, but action in that sphere must be left to God.

As though to offer light relief from the complexities of the moral order and the judgment of God, Job's eyes are directed to a huge creature unaware of ethics. This amphibious colossus can scythe the grass like an ox and take in bushels, but can mount on higher land for food, without disturbing the revels of other beasts (v. 20). In the shade of the lotus-trees he takes his ease where waters comfort his great bulk. Without a care when rivers overflow or Jordan swells, he nevertheless is no easy prey. Those eyes at water level preserve his nostrils from the ring of any master. Mastery belongs to him, as you can see from the massive strength of his loins, his belly muscles, and that tail, "motionless like the short and thick stem of the cedar." It is unusual in Scripture that brute strength, sinews and muscle should be a cause for glorying, yet there is a time for everything, and God can make anything appropriate at His time.

In Psalm 73:22 the word "behemoth" (the plural form of "beast") seems a likely reading in a suggestive context where a man who like Job had been shaken by doubts confesses, "I was as a beast before thee" (See BDB *Oxf. Heb. Lex.*). Although the description of Behemoth given to Job makes modern readers picture a hippopotamus, there are grounds for supposing this lengthy section, like the one on Leviathan which follows, is meant not to be specific in the manner of Chapter 40. There brief and concrete pictures were etched: in the two later sections a more gargantuan creature appears to be presented, behind this "plural of majesty."

LEVIATHAN, UPON EARTH THERE IS NOT HIS LIKE, Chapter 41

41:1-11. A monster unapproachable: no man is so fierce that he dare stir him up. Who then can stand before Me?
12-17. A citadel impregnable, its defenses impenetrable.
18-21. Like the fire-breathing dragon, yet with eyes like the dawn.
22-34. Invincible, he causes consternation. "He is king over all the sons of pride."

To Westerners the crocodile is just a scaly, gruesome animal. People on the Congo River associate it with the uncanny powers that are demonic. Scientific attitudes of mind turn exegesis of this chapter into a series of puzzles, and raise the question why God should be supposed to say all this to Job. To a group in

Central Africa engaged in Bible study, it would "stand out a mile" that here we are being warned against our great Adversary. Since Scripture is given to us, and is not for speculation but for profit, perhaps we ought to imagine the help which many an African preacher of spiritual sensibility could extract from all this.

The quick-fire questions of the first section would amuse an audience by the Zambesi as much as they caught the fancy of the writer of the book, for terror surmounted is close to laughter. There is fun behind the questions of verses 3, 4, 5. Making a covenant with him and making of him a life-long domestic help would make a bunch of African Christians laugh till the tears came—for they see how ludicrous it is to make a contract with Mephistopheles (without having to be a Marlowe or a Goethe). "Will you play with him as with a bird, or make him a pet for thy maidens?" Decidedly this, plus the unforgettable scare-value of verse 8, is a treasury for the men of the River!

On this basis verse 10 is not so unacceptable as learned Western scholars count it, for a man from the River would connect it in utter wholesomeness with the words of Jesus: "But I will forewarn you whom ye shall fear . . ." (Luke 12:5f.). The section ends with God as both the Giver and Possessor of all things, the source of peace for Job and all others who through their weakness discover the secret of victory both over the terrible one and over fear.

"Canst thou draw out Leviathan with a fish hook?" No. But a mere crocodile was enticed ashore by a bait of strong-smelling hippo flesh. Inside the meat was a circular iron bar nine inches long, to which was attached a length of wire cable with its other end around the base of a palm tree. The croc came ashore on a still moonlit night, swallowed the bait, lashed with its tail but would not open its throat. The iron bar was now athwart its throat, and soon the men from neighboring huts made the kill with spears. The writer was a witness after this event, but on more occasions still when "leviathan" was the victor.

To gain dominion over a crocodile is a perilous endeavor, for "who can open the doors of his face?" The scales gave early armorers a pattern, for they appeared impenetrable (verse 15ff). The words of verse 11 do seem unexpected on the Divine lips, but our business is to get the benefit from them. Job had pictured God as his antagonist: who can tell how far this cool and objective description of a creature made by God yet so utterly self-confident and impervious to approach proved a means of showing Job how far astray he had gone in his harsh thoughts of God? There was another one who was Job's adversary.

The chaos monster responsible for resistance to God in early times was a familiar item in popular belief, as 3:8 reminded us. The sneezings of leviathan cause flashes of light, and burning torches go out of his mouth and smoke from his nostrils. It is not the realm of nature that God is describing as in the graphic descriptions of Chapter 39. It is someone with heart firm as the nether millstone. When he raiseth himself up, the mighty are afraid. He counteth iron as straw, maketh the deep to boil. Upon earth there is not his like, made without fear. One thing is clear: Job was now quite certain that this grisly creature was all too like the imaginings to which he himself had given expression, asking himself, "Could this be God?" Leviathan was all too like the spectres of the mind from which Job had suffered such anguish. Impervious? Unapproachable? Causing consternation? Job's poisoned mind had dwelt on pictures just like this. Early in the next chapter we shall hear him declare, "But now, now I know who is my Friend, and how I have distorted His image."

"BETTER THAN AT YOUR BEGINNING," Chapter 42

42:1-6. "I had heard of Thee. . . . Now mine eye seeth thee."
7-17. Epilogue: the vindication of Job, his priestly intercession, the pardon of his friends, and a double peace as great as his prosperity.

Israel's prophets sharply challenged the complacent national expectations of what would happen when God appears to judge the earth. Unsparingly they exposed men's comfortable notions about God's inevitable approval. God, they showed, is totally beyond the perception of the egotist or the jingoist. Only the broken-hearted penitent knows how great He is.

Once again Job's experience runs parallel to that of the great prophets, for God made him a seer. "Now mine eye seeth Thee." There is no temple shaken to its foundations and filled with smoke, as in young Isaiah's vision of the Holy One. No Divine attribute is singled out, nor is the seeing described as sight. But he is given an assurance that comes from immediate confrontation and knowledge. God, not against him but *for* him! How this transforms Job's reading of the Divine omnipotence! "I know that Thou canst do all things," but the purposes God cherishes are now seen as transfigured. Love and goodness has all-needed power to achieve God's wise designs. It is all too wonderful, and what a bungler Job had been at reading those actions and ways of God! He loathed the words he had spoken, for the words condemned the mind that conceived them. Twice therefore Job recalls the words God first addressed to him (38:2, 3). Dust and ashes, as at Nineveh (Jonah 3:6), formed the place suited to his grief. "I repent": that is the pre-condition of living faith.

Job's mental state has often been diagnosed as marked by opposites, and so it is again. Rapturous amazement at God's goodness is succeeded or accompanied by the sharpened pain of self-knowledge. Christ has shown this to be the basis of all beatitude, the twin pillars at the entrance to the house of God. "I adore. . . . I abhor."

The patriarch is reckoned to have been seventy when his calamities broke upon him. The Epilogue tells us that he lived for twice seventy more years in the enjoyment of this profound intimacy with God (v. 16). A beautiful touch of poetic justice!

The prose narrative which concludes the book is true to the Prologue and to the general trend of the discussion and also to the Divine unveiling. Glimpses and intuitions of a life beyond the grave had been given to Job, and these remain a permanent contribution to the unfolding revelation of God, but God had not added to or confirmed Job's pioneering words. Till the end there is every reason to believe that Job fully expected death to overtake him. His vindication therefore did occur on earth, and the return of prosperity was suited to the stage of knowledge in that time. Dying old and full of days means that the happy reversal of his fortunes was given to his contemporaries who had wrongly despised him, given in terms they could understand. And Job retained his great intuitions.

What is more important than outward prosperity and a catalog of it in sheep and camels is the reconciliation God effected between Job and his critics. Job had been rebuked (40:2, 6-9) and had since then gone deeper in discernment of the nature of God. More sharply aware of his gross misjudgement of God, he was standing more nearly on the level with Eliphaz, Bildad, and Zophar. There was no gloating therefore when he heard Eliphaz condemned. Astonished at the verdict on himself, Job must have been impressed by the serious view of the transgression of the men who spoke unrighteously for God. Seven bullocks and seven rams is a very large burnt-offering (cp. Balak in Num. 23:4; the nation Israel in Ezek. 45:22-25). Very significant here is the further instruction, "and my servant Job shall pray for you: for him will I accept."

Reconciliation is God's work, God's gift. But pardon is the most dynamic of gifts. It creates a disposition to pardon others. The intercession of Job is introduced with a striking phrase: "him will I accept." The three friends did as they were told, "and the Lord accepted Job." This is only another of numerous reasons for agreeing that the Book of Job reads like "a first draft of the gospel story." The one who longed for a Mediator was invited to act himself as a mediator.

"And the Lord turned the captivity of Job, when he prayed for his friends" (v. 10).

This brings the most fitting conclusion of all. Nothing under heaven could be more sad than wasted sorrow. But Job's was not wasted. At great cost to him, his friends benefitted and became men of new and wider hearts. In this, too, Job's experience is paralleled in the Apostle Paul. Paul's least responsive, least appreciative congregation surely was that in Corinth. If any Christians humiliated Paul and broke his heart, it was the cocksure saints in Corinth—yet, as Dr. John A. Hutton writing to modern pastors remarked, when they broke his heart, "God entered through the breach."

In the decayed little town of Corinth stands in Apostle Paul Street a cathedral of the Greek Orthodox Church. At the front inside the church, down on the ground in the reserved space near the altar, stands a little wooden plaque with this inscription: "The seal of mine apostleship are ye in the Lord." The complete verse says, "If to others I am not an apostle, yet at least I am to you; for the seal of mine apostleship are ye in the Lord" (I Cor. 9:2).

Not Philippi, not Thessalonica, but Corinth was the seal of Paul's apostleship. Astonishing! Heartbreak House was Heaven's seal on his life's work. And so it was with Job. "My servant Job"—God calls him by this wonderful name four times to the friends in Chapter 42, as He had proudly spoken of him to Satan. And the friends became the first seal of Job's authentic apostolàte from God. This is the book's conclusion in its widest setting, for the Bible's message throughout is reconciliation, and what it cost, and costs.

One of Job's most memorable sayings is surely that in Chapter 19:9, spoken when he was utterly emptied out: "He hath stripped me of my glory, and taken the crown from my head." Discredited, disrobed, discrowned, Job was nearest to the Saviour's experience just then. But like the Saviour, Job shall see his seed, he shall prolong his days. Like Paul he will see his spiritual children, and astonished he will say, "For what is our hope, or joy, or crown of rejoicing? Are not even ye, before our Lord Jesus Christ at his coming?"